4/08

THE OPRAH MAGAZINE COOKBOOK

WITH AN INTRODUCTION BY OPRAH WINFREY

175 DELICIOUS RECIPES TO SAVOR WITH FRIENDS & FAMILY

HYPERION

NEW YORK

ISBN: 978-1-4013-2260-1

O, The Oprah Magazine

Founder and Editorial Director: **Oprah Winfrey**
Editor in Chief: **Amy Gross**
Editor at Large: **Gayle King**
Design Director: **Carla Frank**
Photo Director: **Jennifer Crandall**
Production Director: **Kristen Rayner**
Associate Editor: **Brooke Kosofsky Glassberg**
Assistant Photo Editor: **Kathy Nguyen**

Hearst Books
VP, Publisher: **Jacqueline Deval**

Contributors
Project Management: **Chisomo Kalinga and Mary Goodbody**
Designer: **Tanya Ross-Hughes/Hotfoot Studio**

"Tomato–Roasted Garlic Soup," "Barley Risotto with Mushrooms & Tenderloin of Beef":
First published in *O, The Oprah Magazine* January 2003
From CONSCIOUS CUISINE by Cary Neff © 2005, used with permission by Sourcebooks Inc.

"Pumpkin Soup with Crispy Sage Leaves," "Tangy Autumn Greens," "Two Skillet Roasted Herbed Chicken with Oven Fries": First published in *O, The Oprah Magazine* December 2003 & June 2004
© 2005 From HOMEGROWN: PURE AND SIMPLE by Michel Nischan,
permission of Chronicle Books, LLC.

"Spicy Grilled Snapper with Lemongrass & Ginger":
First published in *O, The Oprah Magazine* October 2004
© 2003 From TASTE: PURE AND SIMPLE by Michel Nischan, permission of Chronicle Books, LLC.

"Beet-Ginger Chutney," "Mango Couscous," "Lemon-Olive Chicken," "Callaloo":
First published in *O, The Oprah Magazine* September 2006
© 2006 From THE SOUL OF A NEW CUISINE by Marcus Samuelsson.
Reprinted with permission of John Wiley & Sons, Inc.

"Caramelized Onion & Bacon Tart," "Lemon Curd Cheesecake":
First published in *O, The Oprah Magazine* November 2005
© 2005 From RECIPES: A COLLECTION FOR THE MODERN COOK by Susan Spungen.
Photographs © by Maria Roblado. Foreword © 2005 by Martha Stewart.
Reprinted by permission of HarperCollins Publishers.

"Edna Lewis's Famous Coconut Lane Cake": First published in *O, The Oprah Magazine* July 2005
From THE GIFT OF SOUTHERN COOKING by Edna Lewis and Scott Peacock with David Nussbaum
© 2003 by Edna Lewis and Scott Peacock.
Used by permission of Alfred A. Knopf, a division of Random House, Inc.

"Spicy Shrimp with Basil," "Roasted Beets with Ginger," "Pumpkin Applesauce Muffins":
First published in *O, The Oprah Magazine* February 2005
From SPICES OF LIFE by Nina Simonds © 2005 by Nina Simonds.
Used by permission of Alfred A. Knopf, a division of Random House, Inc.

"Banana Pudding": First published in *O, The Oprah Magazine* October 2004
From HALLELUJAH! THE WELCOME TABLE by Maya Angelou
© 2004 used by permission of Random House, Inc.

"Rib Eye Steaks with Cornmeal-Fried Onion Rings":
First published in *O, The Oprah Magazine* October 2006
From THE BAREFOOT CONTESSA COOKBOOK by Ina Garten, © 1999 by Ina Garten.
Foreword © by Martha Stewart. Photographs © 1999 by Melanie Acevedo.
Used by permission of Clarkson Potter/Publishers, a division of Random House, Inc.

"Cranberry Cobbler": First published in *O, The Oprah Magazine* January 2005
From INSPIRED BY INGREDIENTS by Bill Telepan and Andrew Friedman
© 2004 used by permission of Simon & Schuster.

Hyperion books are available for special promotions, premiums, or corporate training. For details contact Michael Rentas, Proprietary Markets, Hyperion, 77 West 66th Street, 12th Floor, New York, New York 10023, or call 212-456-0133.

FIRST EDITION

1   3   5   7   9   10   8   6   4   2

Traditional Pavlova
(recipe on page 260)

CONTENTS

Have a Seat at My Table
by Oprah Winfrey

Nobody has ever mistaken me for Julia Child (though I do a pretty decent corn fritter), but even if my culinary skills leave a little something to be desired, I definitely believe in the mystical, magical, healing power of a good home-cooked meal. Is there anything better than walking through your front door and being greeted by the garlicky scent of an old-fashioned pot roast getting fall-apart-on-the-fork tender as it roasts in your oven, or the brown-sugared breeze that floats by whenever there's a peach pie cooling on the kitchen counter? Food—sensuous, lush, and abundant—nourishes the body, revives the spirit, turns strangers into friends, and creates memories that last long after all the pots and pans have been scoured and put away.

So when I began to do a magazine of my own, I knew I wanted recipes that rely on the quality of their ingredients, stories that reflect the culture of a country or the life of a cook, and photographs that leap off the page and make your mouth water. I wanted dishes—some very rich, some very healthy, all very doable—from everywhere. And I wanted to tap into the imaginations of the most creative people (whether four-star chefs or just plain fabulous cooks) ever to put on an apron.

We got Marcus Samuelsson to dazzle us with a bright green callaloo soup and a mellow mango jalapeño couscous. We got Art Smith to share his great-great-grandmother's melt-in-your-mouth 12-layer chocolate cake recipe, Nina Simonds to bake up a batch of pumpkin applesauce muffins that must be the reason God invented coffee, Govind Armstrong to devise a show-stopping Thanksgiving, and Bobby Flay to mix up a cactus pear margarita so enticing, I promise you'll be asking for another round before your second sip.

This cookbook is a compilation of flavors and ideas, exotic places and inspiring traditions, technique, instinct, and of course sublime, delectable, delicious food! Broth is infused with mint and ginger, focaccia is studded with caramelized onion and rosemary, lamb chops are rubbed with ripe orange zest, salmon is brined with maple, tea is brewed with fresh lime and honey, pecans are dusted with cinnamon, ribs mingle with balsamic vinegar and fresh basil, asparagus is broiled with

I definitely believe in the mystical, magical, healing power of a good home-cooked meal.

miso and ginger, a dollop of cilantro cream enlivens a rich cauliflower and apple soup, and cumin meets coconut. And then we invited some of our special friends, who are absolutely passionate about food, to share their favorite culinary memories.

On some pages you'll find that the silver is polished, the crystal is sparkling, the candles are lit, and the champagne is poured. On others, the picnic basket is packed, the iced tea is brewing in the summer sun, and the Frisbee is flying. But whether it's a formal sit-down in the dining room, a casual brunch on the patio, or leftovers in the kitchen, the food, however wonderful, is actually only a supporting player. The starring roles go to the people with whom you share this food.

Let's face it—thanks to the portable DVD player, we can now watch TV in our cars while chatting on our cell phones and receiving e-mails on our BlackBerrys. We can live with people but go days on end without ever making eye contact. We can meet friends at the latest hot spot and then shout to be heard over the scene at the bar. Somehow, dinner has become something we pop in the microwave and gulp down at the sink while signing off on homework and sorting through our mail.

I believe we can do a whole lot better than that and I believe we all deserve better. More than anything else, these dishes are meant to inspire you to bring together your friends, your family.

So here's to the people you love, excellent conversation, lots of laughs, the occasional glass of champagne for no particular reason, and meals you wish would last forever. Here's to life!

Oprah

Fried Green Tomato Salad with Homemade Ranch Dressing
(recipe on page 37)

Chapter 1

APPETIZERS & SALADS

Gazpacho Granita

Chef: Nadia Roden

So much prettier than guacamole, this frozen treat is composed of tiny crystals of potent tomato ice paired with a crisp chopped salad.

GRANITA
2 pounds ripe sweet tomatoes, peeled
1 Tbsp. sugar
1 garlic clove, finely chopped
¼ cup finely chopped fresh basil
2 Tbsp. fresh lemon juice
2 tsp. coarsely ground pepper
¾ tsp. salt

DRESSING
¼ cup extra-virgin olive oil
3 Tbsp. white wine vinegar
¼ tsp. salt
¼ tsp. freshly ground pepper

SALAD
1 red bell pepper, finely diced
1 green bell pepper, finely diced
1 cucumber, peeled, seeded, and finely
  diced
½ red onion, finely diced

1 To make granita: Quarter tomatoes and puree in a food processor with sugar and garlic. Strain puree through a sieve to discard seeds. Stir in basil, lemon juice, pepper, and salt.

2 Let mixture chill in refrigerator at least 20 minutes to allow flavors to develop.

3 Freeze granita as directed at right.

4 To make dressing: Whisk together all ingredients until blended.

5 To assemble salad: In a large bowl combine all ingredients; add dressing and toss to coat. Spoon granita on center of serving dishes. Arrange salad evenly around each.

Makes 4 to 6 servings.

■ **CLASSIC GRANITA METHOD**
Recommended technique
Pour the granita mixture into a wide and shallow container, such as a stainless steel baking dish (the shallower the container, the quicker the granita will freeze).

Cover with a lid, foil, or plastic wrap. Freeze the mixture 1 to 2 hours, until it is solid around the edges. Take the container out of the freezer and scrape the ice with a fork, mixing it from the edges into the center.

Repeat this scraping and mixing process every 30 minutes or so (at least three times) until the entire mixture has turned into small, sequined ice flakes. When ready to serve, "rake" with a fork to loosen the granita and spoon into serving dishes.

■ **QUICK GRANITA METHOD**
Note: This method is faster, but the granita will have a different texture—less icy and more slushy.
Pour the granita mixture into ice trays, cover with plastic wrap, and allow to freeze solid. Process the cubes in a food processor when you're ready to serve.

10

Seared Sea Scallops with Spicy Clementine Dipping Sauce

Chef: Debra Ponzek

Serve these scallops as hors d'oeuvres with this seductive sauce.

DIPPING SAUCE

4 cups fresh-squeezed clementine
   juice, or orange juice
2 tsp. ancho chili powder
Finely grated zest and juice of 1 lime
6 Tbsp. (¾ stick) butter, cut into 8
   pieces

SCALLOPS

½ cup extra-virgin olive oil
40 large sea scallops, patted dry
Salt and freshly ground pepper

1 To make sauce: In a medium saucepan over high heat, bring clementine juice, chili powder, and lime zest and juice to a boil. Reduce heat and simmer 1 hour; mixture should be thickened and syrupy.

2 Remove from heat and whisk in butter, one piece at a time, until incorporated.

3 In a large skillet over high heat, heat 2 Tbsp. olive oil until smoking. Season scallops with salt and pepper. Cook 10 scallops 1 to 2 minutes per side, until dark golden brown. Remove to paper towels and drain. Repeat with remaining oil and scallops in 3 batches. Serve scallops hot with warm sauce.

Makes 40 scallops.

Crushed Potato with Smoked Salmon, Caviar, & Chives

Chef: Daniel Boulud

We can't think of a better group of ingredients: potatoes, smoked salmon, caviar, and chives. Did we mention the caviar? Sublime!

1 cup coarse sea salt

2 large Yukon Gold potatoes (about 14 ounces each), scrubbed and patted dry

2 Tbsp. unsalted butter

2 Tbsp. extra-virgin olive oil

Salt and freshly ground pepper

1 Tbsp. finely chopped chives, plus additional chives for garnish

4 ounces sliced smoked salmon, cut into 1-inch diamonds

1 ounce of sevruga or osetra caviar*

*Caviar and smoked salmon can be purchased at most specialty food stores or ordered via the Internet at www.danielnyc.com.

1 Preheat oven to 425°. Spread sea salt evenly on the bottom of a baking sheet. Place potatoes on top of salt and bake 45 to 50 minutes, or until tender when pierced with a knife.

2 Set potatoes aside to cool and discard salt. Peel potatoes while still quite warm. Place them in a bowl with butter and olive oil. Add salt and pepper to taste. Mash potatoes or crush with fork (they should still be chunky). Stir in chives.

3 To serve: Place a small mound of warm, crushed potato on a Chinese soupspoon or nonmetallic tablespoon. Top with smoked salmon and a dab of caviar. Garnish with chive pieces.

Makes approximately 36 canapés.

14

Roasted Potatoes with Chives, Bacon, & Maytag Blue Cheese

Created by Andre Walker

You can't eat only one of these potato hors d'oeuvres. They're that good.

12 small Yukon Gold potatoes
2 tsp. plus ⅛ tsp. salt
1 tsp. extra-virgin olive oil
⅛ tsp. freshly ground pepper
½ cup crumbled Maytag blue cheese
4 slices applewood-smoked bacon,
   cooked until crisp and crumbled
1 Tbsp. minced chives

1 Preheat oven to 350°. Place potatoes in a large saucepan. Cover with cold water; bring to a boil. Add 2 tsp. salt; cook until tender, about 20 minutes. Drain. Once cooled, slice a small piece from the top and the bottom of each potato. Transfer to a medium bowl; toss with oil, remaining ⅛ tsp. salt, and pepper.

2 Place potatoes on a baking sheet. With a paring knife, score top of each potato. Top each with equal amounts of blue cheese and bacon. Bake until cheese melts, 5 to 7 minutes. Sprinkle with chives and serve.

Makes 12 servings.

15

At the Table with Colin Cowie
THE PERFECT HOST

Entertaining is not about making an impression, says this internationally known event and party planner. Instead, it's about being welcoming and calm and making your guests feel comfortable.

Colin Cowie, renowned for devising spectacular parties, has orchestrated some of the biggest and most elaborate bashes in the world, including events for Oprah, Jennifer Lopez, Tom Cruise, Lisa Kudrow, Kelsey Grammer, and Michael Jordan. His weddings are legendary; his charity galas are magnificent. And on the evenings when he is not working, Colin entertains at home. He is the author of five style and entertaining books, most recently *Colin Cowie Chic: The Guide to Life As It Should Be*.

"I have people over nearly every night," he says, "and it's never about impressing them. It's about having a relaxed evening with interesting people. I don't entertain in restaurants because, let's face it, at the end of the day who wants to make choices? It's far more pleasant to entertain at home."

Colin loves the casual world we now inhabit and says his at-home parties are apt to take place around a big table in his New York City loft kitchen. That doesn't mean he has forsaken the finer things in life. On the contrary. "We get to do it all now," he happily explains. "Your presentation can still be chic and stylish and elegant, even in the relaxed environment of your own kitchen."

He reassures the home cook not to be intimidated by the icons of entertaining. "You don't have to perform," he advises. "You don't have to be perfect."

He recommends that when you entertain, you dim the lights, take out the candles, put on music, and greet your guests with a smile. He almost always offers his company a special cocktail and limits the cocktail hour to 45 minutes or an hour, tops. Dinner, he says, should last about one and a half hours. This way, the party moves and no one feels hungry or restless.

When it comes to the menu, Colin serves uncomplicated meals. He relies on organic and regionally grown produce whenever possible and has found gluten-free pasta and low-carb bread in local markets that say "comfort food" without the guilt.

"Cooking for your friends is not about cooking from scratch," he says. "It's not about chopping and dicing. It's about being resourceful. Select a good bakery, buy olives and cheeses from the market. Don't try to make it all yourself."

Inviting friends into your home is an intimate gesture, and when you do so, use your most cherished possessions and share their beauty with your guests. Colin says he learned this the hard way when he lost some of his most valuable—and valued—glassware in 1994 during the Northridge earthquake in Los Angeles before he had the opportunity to enjoy it.

Finally, he encourages everyone to jump in and invite their friends over, whether it's a very small supper or a more formal dinner party. "Do your best," he says. "It is more than good enough!"

> "I have people over nearly every night, and it's never about impressing them. It's about having a relaxed evening with interesting people."

Colin Cowie's Recipes
- **Sausage Rolls with Worcestershire Sauce** (page 17)
- **Vodka-Espresso Cocktail** (page 46)
- **Brown Rice Risotto and Variations** (page 203)
- **Chocolate Pots de Crème with Vanilla Ice Cream** (page 261)

16

Sausage Rolls with Worcestershire Sauce

Chef: Colin Cowie

These are always a hit—who can resist a warm sausage roll? And the fact that they can be prepared ahead makes them a double winner.

¾ pound lean ground pork or veal
¾ cup finely diced boiled potato
1 small onion, finely chopped
2 Tbsp. chopped fresh parsley
1 tsp. dried sage
½ tsp. salt
½ tsp. freshly ground pepper
¼ tsp. crushed red pepper flakes
One (17¼-ounce) package frozen
 puff pastry sheets, thawed
Flour, for dusting
1 large egg, beaten
1 cup Worcestershire sauce

1 Preheat oven to 350°. To make piping bag, snip 1 corner from a plastic food bag with scissors to make about a ¾-inch opening.

2 Combine pork, potato, onion, parsley, sage, salt, pepper, and pepper flakes in a bowl; transfer sausage mixture to bag.

3 Unfold 1 pastry sheet; following fold marks, cut the sheet into 3 rectangles. Cut each rectangle in half lengthwise to make 6 strips. On a lightly floured surface, roll out each strip into a 12" x 2½"-inch rectangle. Pipe sausage mixture along 1 long edge of each strip. Lightly brush opposite edge with egg. Starting at edge with sausage mixture, roll up each strip, gently pressing egg-brushed edge to seal.

4 With a sharp knife, cut each log crosswise into eight (1½-inch-thick) rolls. Arrange rolls, seam side down, on a broiler pan; brush top with egg. Repeat with remaining pastry and sausage mixture.

5 Bake until golden and cooked through, 30 to 35 minutes. Serve warm with Worcestershire sauce for dipping.

Makes 96 rolls.

17

Crostini with Wild Mushrooms & Mozzarella

Chef: Mollie Ahlstrand

An elegant and delicious first course, these rich-tasting crostini also make a lovely light lunch or supper.

2 Tbsp. extra-virgin olive oil

2 garlic cloves, chopped

1 pound button or wild mushrooms (such as porcini, cremini, shiitake) with stems removed, chopped

¼ cup white wine

½ tsp. salt

¼ tsp. freshly ground pepper

24 small (½-inch-thick) slices country-style bread (preferably ciabatta), toasted

1 pound fresh salted buffalo mozzarella, cut into 24 slices

2 Tbsp. chopped fresh Italian parsley

1 Preheat oven to 375°. In a 12-inch nonstick skillet, heat olive oil over medium-high heat. Sauté garlic until fragrant, about 30 seconds. Add chopped mushrooms and sauté 3 to 4 minutes. Pour in wine; increase heat to high and cook, stirring, until liquid evaporates, about 5 minutes. Mix in salt and pepper.

2 Arrange bread on a large country-style bread baking sheet. Top each piece with a slice of mozzarella. Bake 5 to 7 minutes, until cheese is melted.

3 Top crostini with mushroom mixture; sprinkle with parsley. Serve warm.

Makes 6 servings.

Cornbread Bruschetta with Fresh Corn Salsa

Chef: Rori Trovato

What a surefire appetizer! Make this an hour or so ahead of time—but no earlier—for the best flavor.

CORNBREAD

2 Tbsp. bacon fat or vegetable shortening
1 ¾ cups cornmeal
1 tsp. baking soda
1 tsp. baking powder
1 ½ tsp. salt
2 eggs
2 cups buttermilk

2 red bell peppers

SALSA

2 ears corn, kernels removed
1 Tbsp. fresh lemon juice
1 Tbsp. extra-virgin olive oil
1 tsp. minced garlic
1 Tbsp. minced cilantro
1 tsp. minced jalapeño (optional)
Salt and freshly ground pepper

½ cup sour cream

1 To make cornbread: Position rack on top third of oven and preheat to 450°. Rub bacon fat on bottom and sides of a 9" x 13" baking dish or a large cast-iron frying pan. In a large bowl, combine dry ingredients. In a small bowl, mix eggs and buttermilk. Pour over dry ingredients and blend. Heat baking dish in oven until fat is very hot, then pour cornmeal mixture into pan. Bake 15 to 20 minutes, or until golden brown. Remove from oven and cool on a rack 10 minutes. Cut into 1" x 2" pieces or small wedges.

2 Meanwhile, roast peppers over an open flame until blackened. Place in a bowl and cover with plastic wrap. When cool enough to handle, remove skin with your fingers, wetting your hands in cool water to ease the process. Remove stems and seeds and slice peppers into thin strips.

3 To make salsa: Combine corn, lemon juice, olive oil, garlic, cilantro, and jalapeño; season with salt and pepper.

4 Spread a thin layer of sour cream on cornbread. Top with roasted pepper slices and corn salsa.

Makes 8 servings.

Prosciutto di Parma–Black Pepper Quesadillas with Rosemary Oil

Chef: Bobby Flay

The flavored oil adds an herbaceous finish to the prosciutto and cheese quesadillas.

ROSEMARY OIL

1 cup extra-virgin olive oil
¼ cup fresh rosemary leaves
¼ cup coarsely chopped chives
Salt and freshly ground pepper

QUESADILLAS

Twenty-four (6-inch) flour tortillas
1 ¼ pounds fresh mozzarella, shredded
1 small red onion, finely sliced, rinsed
   and dried
2 to 3 tsp. coarsely ground black pepper
Salt and freshly ground pepper
Olive oil
½ cup grated Parmesan cheese
32 very thin slices prosciutto di Parma

1 Combine the oil, rosemary, chives, and a pinch each of salt and pepper in a food processor and process until smooth. Pour through a fine strainer; store in the refrigerator until ready to use.

2 Preheat the oven to 450°. Place 16 tortillas on an ungreased baking sheet. Spread the mozzarella, onion, and coarse black pepper evenly on each, and season to taste with salt and pepper. Layer the prepared tortillas, 2 per stack, then top with the last 8 tortillas (you will have 3 layers). Brush the quesadillas lightly with olive oil and sprinkle with Parmesan. Bake for 8 to 12 minutes, or until the tortillas are golden brown and the cheese has melted.

3 Cut into quarters, top each with 1 slice of prosciutto, and drizzle with a little rosemary oil.

Makes 8 servings.

ABOVE: **Proscuitto di Parma Quesadillas** and **Cactus Pear Margarita** (recipe on page 44)

21

Baby Greens with Asparagus & Pistachios

Chef: Dan Barber

Light and full of flavor, these greens are simply inspiring!

LEMON OIL

Zest of 1 lemon

1 cup canola oil

4 fresh lemon thyme or thyme sprigs

One (2-inch) piece fresh lemongrass, crushed

LEMON VINAIGRETTE

3 Tbsp. fresh lemon juice

2 Tbsp. lemon oil

¾ tsp. honey

¾ tsp. sherry vinegar

¼ tsp. salt

⅛ tsp. freshly ground pepper

SALAD

1 bunch asparagus, trimmed and cut into 2-inch pieces

1 cup fresh fava beans or frozen lima beans, thawed

8 ounces mixed baby greens

½ cup shelled pistachio nuts, coarsely chopped

1 To make lemon oil: In a small saucepan, combine all ingredients; heat over medium-low heat until oil is hot and small bubbles begin to appear. Transfer to a bowl; cool to room temperature. Cover and let stand at room temperature overnight. Strain before using.

2 To make vinaigrette: In a medium bowl, whisk together all ingredients until blended.

3 To prepare salad: Bring a large pot of lightly salted water to a boil. Add asparagus; cook until just tender, about 2 minutes. Drain in a colander, rinse with cold water until cool, and then drain again. Repeat with beans, cooking about 1 minute before draining.

4 In a large bowl, combine greens, pistachios, asparagus, and beans. Add vinaigrette and toss. Serve immediately.

Makes 6 servings.

Mint & Pea Hummus with Pita Bread

Chef: Rori Trovato

Everyone loves hummus, and when you stir in the bright
flavor of mint, it's more appealing than ever.

1 Tbsp. olive oil

3 small leeks, thoroughly washed and
   chopped, green parts removed

4 cups shelled peas (fresh or frozen)

¾ cup vegetable or chicken broth

2 Tbsp. tahini (sesame seed paste)

2 Tbsp. chopped mint

1 tsp. kosher salt, plus more to taste

½ tsp. black pepper

6 pitas, cut into wedges and toasted

1 In a large sauté pan, heat olive oil over medium-low heat. Add leeks, cover, and cook until tender, 5 to 7 minutes. Add peas and cook uncovered 8 minutes (5 minutes if using frozen peas). Add broth and cook 3 more minutes.

2 Remove from heat, stir in tahini and mint, and spoon mixture into the bowl of a food processor. Process until fairly smooth. Add salt and pepper, seasoning as desired. Place in a bowl and serve with toasted pita wedges.

Makes 1½ cups.

24

Brussels Sprouts Salad with Almonds & Parmesan

Chef: Colin Cowie

Surprise! You don't cook these brussels sprouts. Instead, slice them very thin
for a splendid salad bursting with freshness and great texture.

1 cup slivered almonds

Three (10-ounce) containers brussels
   sprouts

¼ cup olive oil (or 3 Tbsp. olive
   oil plus 1 Tbsp. truffle oil)

3 Tbsp. fresh lemon juice

2 Tbsp. finely sliced chives

½ tsp. salt

¼ tsp. ground black pepper

3 Tbsp. finely grated Parmesan cheese

1 Preheat oven to 350°. Place almonds on baking sheet. Bake for 10 to 12 minutes or until golden brown. Set aside to cool. Slice brussels sprouts as thinly as possible.

2 In large bowl, whisk together olive oil, lemon juice, chives, salt, and pepper. Add brussels sprouts, almonds, and Parmesan. Toss until combined and serve.

Makes 10 servings.

Mint & Pea Hummus with Pita Bread

Heirloom Tomatoes with Lemon Tahini

Chef: Rozanne Gold

For summer's best salad, tahini, or sesame seed paste, becomes a dreamy dressing when enlivened with lemon zest and freshly squeezed lemon juice.

½ cup tahini (sesame seed paste)
Zest of 2 lemons
5 Tbsp. fresh lemon juice
Salt
8 medium heirloom tomatoes, washed and cut into ¼-inch-thick slices
1 lemon, thinly sliced, for garnish
Freshly ground pepper

1 In the bowl of a food processor, place tahini, half the lemon zest, and lemon juice; pulse to combine.

2 With the motor running, add 7 to 8 Tbsp. cold water and continue to process until mixture is thick and smooth. Add salt to taste, and refrigerate until cold.

3 Bring tahini to room temperature. Arrange tomatoes on a platter in a tight overlapping pattern; drizzle half the tahini over tomatoes. Scatter remaining lemon zest on top. Tuck lemon slices around and between tomatoes. Sprinkle with salt and freshly ground pepper. Serve remaining tahini on the side.

Makes 4 servings.

Stacked Tomato Salad

Chef: Joachim Splichal

Look for only the best tomatoes—juicy and vine-ripened.

⅓ cup extra-virgin olive oil
3 Tbsp. chopped fresh parsley
2 Tbsp. fresh lemon juice
½ tsp. salt
⅛ tsp. freshly ground black pepper
2 bunches arugula (stems removed), washed and spun dry
3 small red tomatoes, trimmed and thickly sliced
3 small yellow tomatoes, trimmed and thickly sliced
1 small red onion, thinly sliced
3 ounces Maytag blue cheese, crumbled

1 Whisk together olive oil, parsley, lemon juice, salt, and pepper in a small bowl.

2 Toss arugula with 3 Tbsp. olive oil mixture.

3 Divide arugula evenly among 6 plates. Top with a stack of several red and yellow tomato slices and garnish with red onion. Sprinkle with blue cheese.

Makes 6 servings.

Heirloom Tomatoes with Lemon Tahini

Panzanella

Chef: Rori Trovato

This salad is peasant food made with day-old bread.
So why does it taste like a royal delicacy?

½ cup extra-virgin olive oil

2 garlic cloves, peeled

1 loaf store-bought or homemade rustic country bread, torn into 1- to 1½-inch chunks

2 Tbsp. good-quality red wine vinegar

1 Tbsp. minced shallot

Pinch of sugar

Salt and freshly ground pepper

2 large tomatoes, cut into ½-inch chunks

1 small red onion, thinly sliced

½ unpeeled hothouse cucumber, cut in half lengthwise, then into ½-inch pieces

½ cup basil leaves, cut into ribbons, plus additional for garnish

1 Preheat oven to 400°. In a small saucepan, heat olive oil over medium-high heat; when oil is hot, add garlic cloves. Remove from heat and set aside until cool. Discard garlic cloves.

2 Toss bread in a large bowl with 2 Tbsp. garlic-infused olive oil. Place on a baking sheet. Toast bread until lightly golden and crispy, about 7 to 10 minutes, turning occasionally.

3 To make vinaigrette: Combine remaining olive oil with vinegar, shallot, sugar, salt, and pepper, and mix well.

4 In a large bowl, toss bread, tomatoes, onion, and cucumber with vinaigrette and basil. Season to taste with salt and pepper. Set aside for 30 minutes before serving. Sprinkle with additional basil.

Makes 6 servings.

Sweet Corn Salad with Black Beans, Scallions, & Tomatoes

Created by Moira Hodgson

When summer corn is at its sweet peak, make this
hearty salad for a picnic or supper on the porch.

8 ears corn on the cob

4 Tbsp. extra-virgin olive oil

2 cups black beans (cooked or
  canned), drained and rinsed

4 scallions, chopped

3 ripe plum tomatoes, seeded and
  chopped

1 red bell pepper, diced

3 Tbsp. red wine vinegar, or to taste

Coarse sea salt and freshly ground
  black pepper

2 Tbsp. chopped cilantro or basil, plus
  whole leaves for garnish

1 Shuck corn. In a shallow baking
pan, stand each cob on its
larger end, holding the tapered
end with your noncutting hand.
Using a sharp knife, slice kernels
off; transfer kernels to a bowl. In a
large frying pan, heat 2 Tbsp. olive
oil and sauté kernels until just
softened, 5 to 6 minutes. Return
corn to bowl and add beans, scallions, tomatoes, and red pepper.

2 In a small bowl, combine vinegar, 1 tsp. salt, ¼ tsp. pepper,
and remaining 2 Tbsp. oil. Pour
onto corn mixture, add cilantro or
basil, and mix well. Adjust seasoning to taste before serving.

Makes 6 to 8 servings.

White Bean Salad with Tomatoes & Crisped Sage

Created by Moira Hodgson

The crisped sage leaves are an unusual and impressive garnish.
For the best flavor, serve at room temperature.

1 pound dry beans (white, navy, or
  cannellini)
Kosher salt and freshly ground black
  pepper
2 garlic cloves, minced
1 Tbsp. Dijon mustard
2 to 3 Tbsp. white wine vinegar
⅓ cup extra-virgin olive oil
6 plum tomatoes (about 1 pound),
  chopped
1 small red onion, diced
Canola or grapeseed oil, for frying
1 bunch sage

1 Place beans in a large pot and fill with just enough water to cover. Simmer until beans are tender, 1 to 1½ hours. Just before they're done cooking, season beans with ½ tsp. salt and ¼ tsp. pepper (if you season any sooner, skins of beans may split and centers may harden). Drain, if necessary, and transfer to a large bowl.

2 Meanwhile, with a mortar and pestle, crush garlic and 1 tsp. salt until a paste forms. Add mustard and mix well. Add vinegar. Gradually whisk in olive oil until a smooth emulsion forms. Pour mixture over beans while still warm. Add tomatoes and onion; toss to coat and set aside.

3 Pour in enough canola or grapeseed oil to cover the bottom of a large skillet and place over medium-high heat until oil is very hot but not smoking. Add sage leaves in 1 layer, sprinkle with salt, and fry lightly until crisp, about 2 minutes. (If leaves are crowded, fry in batches.) With a slotted spoon, remove to a plate covered with paper towels; let drain.

4 Sample salad and adjust seasoning to taste. Sprinkle with sage leaves just before serving.

Makes 6 to 8 servings.

31

Sweet Potato Salad

Chef: Art Smith

Just a few special ingredients added to sweet potatoes
result in an out-of-this-world side dish.

2 large sweet potatoes (about 1¼
  pounds)
2 Tbsp. light mayonnaise
1 Tbsp. Dijon mustard
½ tsp. salt
¼ tsp. coarsely ground black pepper
2 large celery stalks, coarsely chopped
  (about ¾ cup)
½ cup thinly sliced red bell pepper
½ cup coarsely chopped fresh
  pineapple
¼ cup pecans, toasted and coarsely
  chopped
1 small green onion, thinly sliced (about
  2 Tbsp.)
Chopped chives, for garnish

1 Using a fork, prick the sweet potatoes in several places. Microwave them on High about 8 minutes, or until tender, turning over midway through cooking. Cool the potatoes until easy to handle. Peel off the skin and cut into ¾-inch chunks.

2 Meanwhile, in a large bowl, mix the mayonnaise, mustard, salt, and pepper until blended.

3 Add the sweet potato chunks, celery, red pepper, pineapple, pecans, and green onion to the mayonnaise mixture. Toss gently until evenly coated. Sprinkle with the chopped chives.

Makes 4 cups.

Tangy Autumn Greens with Tamari-Roasted Walnuts, Dried Cherries, & Stilton

Chef: Michel Nischan

The walnuts get their elusive flavor from tamari, a soy sauce that adds saltiness but has more character than table salt.

1 Tbsp. tamari

2 tsp. molasses

Pinch of salt plus ¼ tsp.

⅛ tsp. plus ¼ tsp. freshly ground pepper

Pinch of cayenne pepper

1 cup walnut halves

½ cup apple juice

½ cup balsamic vinegar

¾ cup dried cherries

1 tsp. extra-virgin olive oil

9 ounces mixed full-flavored salad greens such as arugula, frisée, dandelion, and mustard

1 small red onion, peeled and thinly sliced

1 cup crumbled Stilton cheese

1 To make walnuts: Preheat oven to 350°. In a small bowl, stir tamari, molasses, a pinch of salt, ⅛ tsp. pepper, and cayenne until blended. Add nuts and toss until coated. With a slotted spoon, transfer walnuts to a wire rack set over a baking sheet and roast about 10 minutes, or until browned. Remove from oven and let cool completely on rack. Set aside.

2 To make dressing: In a 1-quart saucepan, heat apple juice and vinegar over medium heat until mixture boils. Place cherries in a small bowl. Pour hot juice mixture over cherries; allow cherries to marinate and soften, 30 minutes. Strain juice mixture from cherries into the same saucepan. Heat mixture to boiling; simmer 15 to 17 minutes over medium heat, or until juice mixture is reduced to ¼ cup. Transfer juice mixture to a small bowl and blend with oil. Set aside to cool completely.

3 In a large bowl, combine greens, walnuts, red onion, Stilton, ¼ tsp. salt, ¼ tsp. pepper, and marinated cherries. Whisk dressing just before drizzling over salad. Toss salad gently and briefly to prevent cheese from clumping.

Makes 12 servings.

Warm Roasted Vegetable Salad

Chef: Nina Simonds

Vegetables roasted in the oven turn sweet and intense.
The soy-garlic dressing accentuates the flavor.

2 large sweet potatoes, peeled and halved

1 medium acorn squash, halved, seeds removed

2 medium fennel bulbs, trimmed, cut lengthwise into ¼-inch-thick slices

2 medium red onions, cut lengthwise into ¼-inch-thick slices

⅓ cup extra-virgin olive oil

⅓ cup balsamic vinegar

3 Tbsp. minced fresh ginger

3 Tbsp. soy sauce

1 large garlic clove, crushed

2 tsp. sugar

1 Preheat oven to 425°. Cut each sweet potato and squash half into 4 wedges. In a large bowl, combine sweet potatoes, squash, fennel, onions, oil, vinegar, and ginger. Toss to coat.

2 Spray two 15½" x 10½" rimmed baking sheets with nonstick spray. Divide vegetables between baking sheets, spreading in a single layer. Roast until tender and browned, 40 to 50 minutes, turning halfway through cooking time.

3 Meanwhile, in a small bowl, stir together soy sauce, garlic, sugar, and 5 Tbsp. water until sugar dissolves. Arrange vegetables on a serving platter. Spoon soy sauce mixture over vegetables. Serve warm or at room temperature.

Makes 6 servings.

Fried Green Tomato Salad with Homemade Ranch Dressing

Chef: Rori Trovato

Looking for a tasty way to use those green tomatoes from your garden? This salad is one of the best, and the creamy, garlicky ranch dressing is its crowning glory.

DRESSING

1 small garlic clove, minced

1 Tbsp. chopped fresh dill

1 Tbsp. chopped fresh flat-leaf parsley

2 scallions, finely chopped

½ cup buttermilk

⅓ cup sour cream

1 tsp. kosher salt, or more to taste

½ tsp. freshly ground black pepper

TOMATOES

Canola oil, for frying

1 Tbsp bacon fat (optional)

½ cup cornmeal

1 tsp. freshly ground black pepper

2 large egg whites, whisked

2½ pounds unripe (green) tomatoes, cut into ½-inch slices

Kosher salt

SALAD

2½ cups baby arugula, or other baby lettuces

1 Combine dressing ingredients in a sealable container. Shake well; taste and add salt if needed.

2 In a nonstick skillet over high heat, bring ¾ inch canola oil plus bacon fat (if using) to very hot. On a large plate, combine cornmeal and pepper; place egg whites on another large plate. Dip tomato slices first in the egg whites and then in the cornmeal, pressing the cornmeal slightly into the tomato so that each slice is fully coated.

3 Add tomato slices to the oil in batches, taking care not to crowd. Fry until golden brown, 3 to 5 minutes per side. Remove to a paper towel–lined surface and sprinkle with kosher salt. Serve warm on a bed of baby lettuces, drizzled with dressing.

Makes 4 servings.

37

Select tomatoes that are green because they're unripe (and thus firm and tangy), not because they're a variety that stays green even when they're ready to eat.

Beet Salad with Grilled Red Onions, Manouri Cheese, & Kalamata Vinaigrette

Chef: Jim Botsacos

You can take a traditional Greek salad to new heights by adding just a few exotic flavors.

SALAD

4 medium red beets, trimmed
½ cup red wine vinegar
1½ tsp. salt
2 medium red onions, each sliced into ½-inch-thick slices
2 Tbsp. extra-virgin olive oil
¼ tsp. freshly ground pepper
6 cups mesclun
6 ounces Manouri or other mild goat cheese, diced

VINAIGRETTE

2 Tbsp. red wine vinegar
1 Tbsp. olive brine (from jar of kalamata olives)
1 tsp. honey
½ tsp. crushed dried oregano (preferably Greek)
¼ tsp. salt
⅛ tsp. freshly ground pepper
¼ cup extra-virgin olive oil

1 To make salad: In a large saucepan, combine beets, vinegar, 1 tsp. salt, and enough cold water to cover beets by 2 inches; bring to a boil. Reduce heat and cook until tender, 40 to 45 minutes. Cool beets in cooking liquid; peel. Using a handheld slicer, cut beets into ⅛-inch-thick slices. Set aside.

2 Meanwhile, heat a grill or a grill pan. Brush both sides of onion slices with olive oil; sprinkle with pepper and remaining ½ tsp. salt. Grill onions over medium heat until evenly charred and tender, 2 to 3 minutes per side.

3 To make vinaigrette: In a small bowl, whisk together vinegar, brine, honey, oregano, salt, and pepper. Gradually add oil, whisking in a thin, steady stream until blended.

4 Arrange 1 cup greens and ¼ cup cheese on each of 6 plates. Divide the sliced beets and grilled onions equally among the plates and drizzle with vinaigrette.

Makes 6 servings.

38

Pomegranate Daiquiris
(recipe on page 46)

Chapter 2

COCKTAILS & BEVERAGES

At the Table with Susan Spungen
A LUNCHTIME MUSE

Jet-lagged and hungry, Susan Spungen and her then-fiancé (now her husband) arrived in Paris on a weekend morning and went directly to visit an old friend. "It was the only time we could get together," Susan recalls. When they arrived at the large Paris apartment for Sunday lunch it was "like stepping into a dream."

In Europe, she says, Sunday lunch is a time-honored tradition and, at this typical gathering, there were five or six couples and assorted children. The meal was a simple one of osso buco, a green salad, great bread, and amazing cheese and wine, and as the assembled company ate, the afternoon meandered on so that before she knew it, it was six o'clock. Susan and her fiancé left happy, well fed, and filled with a sense of relaxed well-being.

Such can be the glory of the midday meal. Of course this is not always so. Lunch is too often overlooked or rushed, so Susan takes particular care with the meal. During the week, she "makes it at home and looks forward to it all morning." She describes herself as a healthy eater and will pack a salad as well as some protein such as chicken or salmon, which may or may not be left over from the night before. "I like variety at lunch," the cookbook author says. Her salads might include asparagus, beets, or green beans—whatever is fresh and travels well.

If your kitchen is organized and equipped, Susan maintains, lunch is not difficult to transport to work or school. All you need are the right containers and the right food.

Susan is the founding food editor and former editorial director for food at Martha Stewart Living Omnimedia from its launch in 1991 until 2003. Her most recent book, *Recipes: A Collection for the Modern Cook*, published in 2005 by William Morrow, is organized by technique because she believes a significant part of enjoying a meal lies in the cooking—not just in the eating—and she wants her readers to get into the kitchen. She urges home cooks to learn the difference between sautéing and braising, chopping and mincing, grilling and barbecuing, but mostly she wants everyone to create opportunities to sit down and break bread together.

> Weekend lunches can be lovely, short and sweet or languorous get-togethers.

Weekend lunches, she says, can be lovely, short and sweet or languorous get-togethers. Regardless, the meal is relaxed. "What is mundane at dinner can be special at lunch," she says, giving the example of a fantastic sandwich. "All you need is fresh bread, a roasted chicken—even a good rotisserie chicken from the market—and, depending on the season, some good tomatoes and maybe some cheese." The smallest effort makes the meal "incredibly satisfying." She adds that while dinner often is about impressing your guests, lunch is all about making them feel well-cared for. Susan loves dessert, although at lunch she keeps it simple with cookies, fresh fruit, a coffee cake, or perhaps a fruit buckle to end the meal on a sweet note.

When you plan lunch, the food should be easy, she believes. It can be served cold or be a dish that is easy to prepare ahead of time. Part of the meal could be store-bought—Susan suggests relying on a great bakery, a robust olive bar, and a cheese counter. The table should be simple and casual and the host shouldn't feel the pressure he or she might at a dinner party.

What else does Susan like about entertaining at lunch? "You still have the evening free!" she says with a smile.

Susan Spungen's Recipes
- **Caramelized Onion & Bacon Tart** (page 180)
- **Lemon Curd Cheesecake** (page 240)

42

O Fizz

Chef: Olivier Cheng

Dazzle your guests with this colorful all-occasion sparkler!

3 tsp. sugar (or simple syrup)
12 fresh mint sprigs, plus extra
for garnish
3 ounces fresh lime juice
Ice
8 ounces vodka
Cranberry juice
Champagne or sparkling wine
Fresh raspberries, for garnish

For each fizz, add ¾ tsp. sugar, 3 mint sprigs, and ¾ ounce fresh lime juice to a cocktail shaker. Muddle content with a long-handled muddler or bar spoon; add ice to shaker, along with 2 ounces vodka and a splash of cranberry juice. Shake vigorously and strain into a flute. Top the glass with champagne; garnish with a few fresh raspberries and a sprig of mint.

Makes 4 drinks.

Lemon Thyme Martinis

Created by Andre Walker

If you've never thought of infusing a martini with thyme,
you're in for an extremely pleasant surprise.

1 bottle (375 ml) dry vermouth
1 bunch (1 ounce) fresh thyme, several
sprigs set aside
Chilled vodka
Ice
1 bunch lemon verbena

1 To make the infusion: Pour vermouth into a bowl; add thyme. Press thyme into vermouth with a spoon. Cover tightly for 24 hours. Discard thyme.

2 To make one martini: Combine 2 ounces chilled vodka, 2 tsp. thyme-infused vermouth, ice, and a lemon verbena sprig in a cocktail shaker. Shake and strain into a chilled martini glass. Garnish with a fresh lemon verbena sprig and a thyme sprig.

Makes 1 drink.

Cocktails & Beverages

Mango Cocktail

Chef: Colin Cowie

Kick-start the evening with these tangy cocktails spiked with vodka and Cointreau.

¾ cup vodka (preferably Grey Goose)
⅓ cup Cointreau
2 cups mango puree*
¼ cup lime juice
Fresh mango wedges, for garnish

* If you can't find mango puree (often sold in aseptic containers) in your local supermarket, try the frozen puree from www.lepicerie.com.

In a large glass pitcher, combine all ingredients; refrigerate until cold. Serve chilled, in cocktail glasses, garnished with fresh mango wedges.

Makes 6 drinks.

Cactus Pear Margaritas

Chef: Bobby Flay

Mango nectar or thawed cranberry juice concentrate can be substituted for the cactus pear juice, but if you can find it, the margarita will be magical.

8 ounces white (blanco) tequila
4 ounces Cointreau or other orange-flavored liqueur
4 ounces cactus pear juice
2 ounces freshly squeezed lime juice
1 cup ice cubes
Lime wedges, for garnish
Coarse salt (optional), for garnish

1 Place the tequila, Cointreau, cactus pear and lime juices, and ice in a blender and pulse until smooth.

2 If using salt for garnish, rub a lime wedge around the rims of the glasses and dip the rims into a saucer of coarse salt.

3 Divide the mixture among 4 margarita glasses; garnish each with a lime wedge.

Makes 4 drinks.

Mango Cocktail

Pomegranate Daiquiris

Chef: Alison Mesrop

Pomegranate juice is the secret weapon in this magnificent cocktail.

3 ½ cups pomegranate juice
1 ½ cups plain or raspberry-flavored
 light rum
1 cup cassis or cranberry liqueur
⅓ cup fresh lime juice
Ice cubes
Pomegranate seeds, frozen green
 grapes, or kiwi slices, for garnish

1 Combine pomegranate juice, rum, cassis, and lime juice in a large pitcher. Cover and refrigerate until cold, at least 4 hours or up to 1 week ahead.

2 In a blender, combine 1 ½ cups juice mixture and 1 cup ice cubes. Blend until slushy. Pour into large martini or wine glasses; garnish as desired. Repeat with remaining juice.

Makes about 12 drinks.

Vodka-Espresso Cocktail

Chef: Colin Cowie

A suave concoction of vodka, coffee, and coffee liqueurs guaranteed
to get—and keep—the joint jumping.

1 ounce premium vodka (or tequila,
 if you prefer)
1 ounce cold espresso
½ ounce Tia Maria
½ ounce Kahlúa Especial

1 To prepare drink: Pour ingredients into a shaker filled with ice. Shake and strain into a martini glass (or three shot glasses).

2 To serve (optional): Rub the pith of an orange along the rim of each glass. Dip rim into cocoa powder spiked with a dash of cayenne pepper; tap glass to remove excess. Pour drink.

Makes 1 drink.

Irish Coffee

Chef: Colin Cowie

Irish coffee is a perfect way to end the evening. This one is especially divine.

3 cups heavy or whipping cream
7 Tbsp. sugar
1 cup Irish whiskey
6 cups rich, hot brewed coffee
Grated nutmeg or ground cinnamon
   (optional), for garnish

1 In a large mixing bowl, beat cream and 3 Tbsp. sugar until very soft peaks form (consistency should be just pourable). Cover and refrigerate until ready to serve.

2 Heat 8 wineglasses by pouring very hot water into them. Drain water; add 2 Tbsp. whiskey to each glass.

3 Stir remaining 4 Tbsp. sugar into coffee until dissolved. For each drink, fill glass with coffee to within 1¼ inch from top. Hold large spoon upside down over top of glass; gradually pour whipped cream over back of spoon onto coffee (cream should float on top, about 1 inch thick). Sprinkle with nutmeg or cinnamon, if desired.

Makes 8 drinks.

Dark & Stormies

Chef: Alison Mesrop

These are even better with ginger beer ice cubes, but if you haven't the time for them, no worries! Any way you serve it, this is a spectacular drink.

8 cups (64 ounces) ginger beer
4 cups (32 ounces) dark rum
½ cup fresh lime juice, or to taste
Ginger beer ice cubes (see step 2)
Thinly sliced lime, for garnish

1 Stir ginger beer, rum, and lime juice in a pitcher. Serve in tall cocktail glasses with 3 or 4 ice cubes each; garnish with lime.

2 To make ginger beer ice cubes: Pour 8 cups ginger beer into 4 ice cube trays and freeze. Try Barritt's Ginger Beer, available at sodapopstop.com, and Gosling's rum.

Makes about 16 drinks.

Mint Tisane

Created by Peggy Knickerbocker

There's nothing like the soothing digestive qualities of an herbal tea.
Use fresh mint alone or in combination with lemon verbena.

1 bunch fresh mint
1 bunch fresh lemon verbena (optional)
3 to 6 cups boiling water
Sugar to taste (optional)

Place 1 bunch mint and 1 bunch lemon verbena (including stems) in teapot. Pour in boiling water and allow to steep about 5 minutes. Add sugar, if desired. Serve in small Moroccan or other clear tea glasses.

Makes 3 to 6 cups.

Strawberry-Mint Iced Tea

Adapted from Josie's Restaurant & Juice Bar, New York City

Strawberries—a symbol of spring—are delicious enough as they are. But
if you have a little more time, we have a new idea for savoring them.

1 pint fresh strawberries, sliced
8 fresh mint leaves
½ cup fruit juice sweetener*
4 Celestial Seasonings Red Zinger tea bags

*Available in health- and specialty-food stores, or substitute apple or grape juice concentrate or 7 Tbsp. sugar.

1 In a medium saucepan, bring 6 cups water to a boil. Add ¾ pint strawberries and mint. Simmer approximately 6 minutes or until water becomes light red in color.

2 Add fruit juice sweetener and tea bags. Simmer 1 minute.

3 Remove saucepan from heat and allow tea bags to steep 3 to 4 minutes.

4 Strain mixture through a fine sieve and mash strawberries to extract more juice.

5 Cool to room temperature and refrigerate until serving.

6 Pour over ice. Garnish with remaining sliced strawberries.

Makes 6 servings.

Mint Tisane

Fresh Lime & Honey Tea

Chef: Rori Trovato

Soothing and piquant, this lovely tea accomplishes what tea should: It comforts and invigorates at the same time.

3 whole limes
½ cup honey
3 Tbsp. loose black tea or 4 tea bags
4 cups boiling water

1 While applying pressure, roll limes several times on counter to release their juices. Cut into ¼-inch slices and place in a large teapot, reserving 4 slices. Add honey and tea to pot.

2 Pour boiling water over tea and let steep 3 minutes.

3 Garnish teacups with reserved lime slices and pour in hot tea. (If using loose tea leaves, pour through a strainer.)

Makes 4 servings.

Watermelon Lemonade

Chef: Rozanne Gold

Adjust the sweetness by experimenting with the amount of honey and lemon.

1½ pounds sliced seedless watermelon, rind removed
Zest of 1 lemon
¾ cup fresh lemon juice
½ cup mild honey (such as orange blossom)
1 ½ cups cold water
1 lemon, thinly sliced, for garnish

1 In the bowl of a food processor, place watermelon and process until very smooth. Strain through a coarse sieve set over a bowl, stirring to push through any pulp. Pour juice into a large pitcher. Add lemon zest.

2 In a bowl, whisk lemon juice and honey until honey dissolves; stir into watermelon juice. Stir in water; cover and refrigerate until very cold. Serve over ice and garnish with lemon slices.

Makes 4 servings.

Fresh Lime & Honey Tea

Classic Hot Chocolate

Adapted from Chocolate Bar, New York City

Forget powdered cocoa mixes. Try the real thing for an over-the-top treat!

2 ounces (½ cup) finely ground (in a coffee grinder) or grated bittersweet chocolate

1 cup milk (for best results, use 2 percent fat or higher)

Whipped cream or marshmallows, for garnish

In a saucepan, combine the chocolate and milk, and bring to a boil, stirring constantly. Boil 1 minute. Garnish with whipped cream or marshmallows. Serve immediately.

Makes about 1 cup.

Mexican Hot Chocolate

Chef: Rori Trovato

Gorgeous, frothy Mexican hot chocolate adds a rich rush of pleasure to the dreariest day.

3 ounces unsweetened chocolate or Mexican chocolate tablets*

½ cup sugar

2 Tbsp. instant espresso granules

1¼ tsp. ground cinnamon

Pinch of salt

1 Tbsp. finely grated orange zest

4 cups milk

½ tsp. almond extract

Cinnamon sticks, for garnish

Sweetened whipped cream (optional)

*Mexican chocolate tablets can be purchased at www.mexgrocer.com.

1 Combine chocolate, sugar, espresso granules, cinnamon, salt, orange zest, and 1½ cups water in a medium saucepan over low heat. Stir until chocolate is melted and mixture is smooth. Bring to a boil, then reduce heat and simmer 5 minutes.

2 Stir in milk and almond extract; reheat but do not boil. Remove saucepan from stove; whisk hot chocolate until foamy.

3 Pour into mugs. Garnish with cinnamon sticks and top with whipped cream, if desired.

Makes 4 to 6 servings.

Mexican Hot Chocolate

Tomato Sandwich
(recipe on page 79)

Chapter 3

SOUPS & SANDWICHES

Classic Clam Chowder

Adapted from Chatham Bars Inn, Cape Cod

Clam chowder. Lobsters. Steamers. Fresh corn. Lots of napkins, bibs, and beer. A clambake celebrates everything that's good about summer, past and present.

2 medium russet potatoes (about 1 pound), peeled and cut into ½-inch cubes

2 Tbsp. unsalted butter

⅔ cup diced white onions

⅔ cup diced celery

½ cup all-purpose flour

Four (6½-ounce) cans chopped clams, juice and clams reserved separately*

Two (8-ounce) bottles clam juice*

1-ounce piece salt pork

1 cup light cream

½ tsp. salt

*Or substitute 1 quart fresh shelled clams and juice and only one (8-ounce) bottle clam juice.

1 Put the potatoes and enough water to cover in a large saucepan; bring to a boil. Reduce heat to a simmer, cover, and cook 10 minutes, until tender; then drain and set aside.

2 In another large saucepan, melt the butter over medium heat. Add the onions and celery; sauté until tender, about 4 minutes. Stir in the flour. Reduce heat to low and cook 10 minutes, until the flour is just golden; remove from heat.

3 In the same pan used for the potatoes, mix the clam juice from the drained clams, the bottled clam juice, and the salt pork and bring to a boil. Simmer the mixture 1 minute. Gradually whisk the hot clam juice into the flour-and-vegetable mixture until smooth. Return the pan to medium-high heat. Add the potatoes, cream, and salt; bring to a boil, stirring often. Stir in clams and just heat through, about 1 minute.

Makes 6 servings.

Tomato–Roasted Garlic Soup

Chef: Cary Neff

This light, garlicky update on tomato soup is only slightly harder to make than the canned version.

1 head garlic
½ tsp. extra-virgin olive oil
Salt and freshly ground pepper
1 cup chopped onion
1 cup chopped celery
Four (14½-ounce) cans stewed
    tomatoes, undrained
1 bay leaf
2 tsp. dried basil
1 tsp. dried oregano
1 tsp. dried thyme

1 Preheat oven to 350°. Remove papery skin from garlic, leaving heads intact. Place garlic on a sheet of heavy-duty foil; drizzle with ¼ tsp. olive oil and sprinkle with a pinch of salt and pepper.

2 Loosely wrap foil around garlic, folding foil edges securely. Roast until garlic has softened, about 40 minutes, then transfer to plate. Open carefully and discard foil; let garlic cool.

3 Separate garlic into cloves. Squeeze soft garlic from each clove into a small bowl; set aside.

4 In a large saucepan over medium heat, heat remaining ¼ tsp. olive oil. Add onion, celery, and roasted garlic. Cover and cook until vegetables soften, about 3 minutes. Stir in tomatoes, 1 cup water, bay leaf, basil, oregano, thyme, and ¼ tsp. pepper; bring to a boil. Reduce heat and simmer 15 minutes to blend flavors.

5 Remove bay leaf. In a blender, puree soup in batches until smooth.

Makes 4 servings.

58

Red Pepper & Fennel Soup

Chef: Norma Jean Darden

We like it hot and spicy, but to tame the heat, use only half a pickled cherry pepper. The swirl of white yogurt just before serving makes this soup pretty as a picture.

2 Tbsp. olive oil

3 medium red peppers, seeded and coarsely chopped

1 medium fennel bulb (fronds discarded), coarsely chopped

1 medium onion, diced

1 hot pickled red cherry pepper, seeded and chopped

4 cups (32 ounces) chicken broth

1 cup plain nonfat yogurt

½ tsp. salt

Fresh basil (optional)

1 In a large saucepan, heat olive oil over medium heat. Cook red peppers, fennel, and onion until softened, about 15 minutes. Add cherry pepper and chicken broth and bring mixture to a boil over high heat. Reduce heat to medium and simmer uncovered for 20 minutes.

2 Using a blender and working in small batches, puree soup. Blend ¾ cup yogurt and salt into the last batch.

3 Return soup to saucepan and heat through, over low heat. Do not boil (yogurt will curdle). Garnish with a swirl of remaining yogurt and a little basil, if desired.

Makes 6 servings.

59

Chickpea & Rosemary Soup

Chef: April Bloomfield

This creamy soup reveals unexpected depths.

3 Tbsp. olive oil, plus additional for drizzling

8 garlic cloves, finely chopped

1 Tbsp. minced fresh rosemary leaves

½ tsp. crushed red pepper flakes

Three (15- to 19-ounce) cans chickpeas, rinsed and drained

4 cups chicken broth

2 Tbsp. fresh lemon juice

Sea salt

1 In a large saucepan, heat 3 Tbsp. oil over medium heat. Add garlic, rosemary, and red pepper flakes. Cook, stirring constantly, until garlic starts to brown, about 1 minute. Add chickpeas and cook 2 minutes, stirring constantly. Add broth and bring to a boil. Reduce heat and simmer 30 minutes; let cool slightly.

2 Transfer 1 cup of soup at a time to a blender; cover loosely and puree until just smooth. Return to saucepan. Repeat two more times. Stir lemon juice and salt into soup to taste. Drizzle with olive oil and serve.

Makes 6 servings.

Yellow Velvet Soup with Prawns

Chef: Melissa Kelly

The chunky relish provides the perfect counterpoint to this satiny smooth, rich soup.

PRAWNS

¼ tsp. chili powder

1 tsp. fresh lime juice

2 Tbsp. honey

1 Tbsp. chopped cilantro

6 prawns (jumbo shrimp), peeled and deveined

Salt and freshly ground pepper

SOUP

1 tsp. extra-virgin olive oil

1 medium onion, diced

4 ears fresh corn, kernels removed

2 small yellow squash, coarsely diced

1 tsp. minced garlic

1 bay leaf

2 cups vegetable stock

½ cup heavy cream

Salt and freshly ground pepper

Cilantro sprigs, for garnish

RELISH

1 poblano chili pepper

¼ cup extra-virgin olive oil

3 ears fresh corn, kernels removed

½ small red onion, finely diced (¼ cup)

½ small red bell pepper, finely diced (¼ cup)

½ small yellow bell pepper, finely diced (¼ cup)

½ small green bell pepper, finely diced (¼ cup)

1 small jalapeño pepper, seeds removed and finely diced

1 Tbsp. minced fresh marjoram

¼ cup fresh lime juice

Dash of green Tabasco sauce

Salt and freshly ground pepper

1 To cook prawns: Combine chili powder, lime juice, honey, and cilantro. Add prawns and marinate in chili powder mixture 1 hour. Grill or sauté prawns 2 minutes on each side. Season with salt and pepper to taste.

2 To prepare soup: In a 6-quart saucepan, heat olive oil over medium heat. Add onion and cook until translucent. Add corn kernels and squash, cooking 4 to 5 minutes. Add garlic and bay leaf; cook an additional 2 minutes. Stir in vegetable stock and 2 cups water and bring to a boil. Reduce to a simmer, and cook until vegetables are soft, about 15 minutes. Stir in cream and return to a boil. Season with salt and pepper to taste. Cool 10 minutes. Puree soup in a blender and strain through a sieve. Adjust seasoning.

3 To make relish: Roast poblano in a pan on stovetop or in broiler until completely charred. Place poblano in a paper bag; close bag and let stand 15 minutes. Remove from bag, peel off skin, remove seeds, and dice. Heat 2 Tbsp. olive oil in a large sauté pan over medium heat. Add corn kernels and cook 3 to 4 minutes until corn brightens in color. Drain; set aside to cool. Place diced vegetables in a bowl. Add poblano, remaining olive oil, corn, marjoram, lime juice, and Tabasco. Stir to blend well. Season with salt and pepper to taste.

4 To serve: Ladle hot soup into shallow bowls. Spoon a mound of corn relish into center of each. Place 1 prawn on top of relish. Garnish with sprigs of cilantro.

Makes 6 servings.

Pumpkin Soup with Crispy Sage Leaves

Chef: Michel Nischan

Pumpkin tastes like the holidays! Spread a little cheer
with a steaming bowl of this piquant soup.

3 pounds pumpkin, peeled, seeded, and cut into 1-inch cubes
2 Tbsp. extra-virgin olive oil
Salt and freshly ground pepper
1 medium Vidalia or other sweet onion, sliced ¼-inch thick
6 cloves garlic, peeled and halved lengthwise
½ cup plus 2 tsp. grapeseed oil
5 cups vegetable or chicken stock
2 cinnamon sticks
3 green cardamom pods or 3 tsp. ground cardamom
1 small Thai or jalapeño chili pepper, seeded and chopped
13 fresh sage leaves

1 Preheat oven to 350°. In a large bowl, toss together pumpkin and olive oil; season with salt and pepper to taste. Spread evenly on 2 large baking sheets. Roast 25 minutes, shaking pans occasionally and switching the positions of pans halfway through.

2 In a separate bowl, toss together onion, garlic, and 2 tsp. grapeseed oil. Add to baking sheets. Roast 15 minutes longer, or until pumpkin and onion are tender. Keep an eye on garlic and turn, if necessary, to keep from burning. Transfer to a small Dutch oven or a large saucepan.

3 Add stock, cinnamon, cardamom, and chili. Bring to a simmer over high heat, reduce heat, and simmer, covered, 20 to 25 minutes, or until pumpkin begins to soften.

4 Discard cinnamon sticks and cardamom pods. Transfer soup to a blender or food processor and blend until smooth. Mince one sage leaf and add to soup. Season with salt and pepper to taste. Keep warm.

5 Meanwhile, in a small skillet, heat remaining ½ cup grapeseed oil to 350°, or until a sage leaf sizzles when added to oil. Fry remaining sage leaves, 4 at a time, turning once, until crisp, about 1 minute total; do not brown. Drain on paper towels and season lightly with salt and pepper.

6 Transfer soup to serving bowls and garnish with crispy sage leaves.

Makes 12 servings.

Avgolemono Soup

Created by Moira Hodgson

Lemon is the star ingredient in this classic Greek chicken soup.

1 quart chicken broth, preferably
   homemade
½ cup orzo (or long-grain rice)
2 large eggs
3 Tbsp. fresh lemon juice (about 1
   lemon)
1 tsp. grated lemon zest
Sea salt and freshly ground white
   pepper to taste
2 Tbsp. chopped dill or parsley

1 In a large saucepan, bring chicken broth to a boil. Add orzo; cover, reduce heat, and simmer 10 minutes, or until orzo is al dente. (If using rice, add another cup of chicken broth. Simmer according to package directions, or until grains are tender.) Do not drain; set aside.

2 In a bowl, beat eggs until thick. Whisk in lemon juice and zest. Gradually add ½ cup hot broth from saucepan, whisking constantly. Add 2 more ½ cups of broth, whisking after each addition.

3 Pour mixture back into saucepan and reheat, stirring with a wooden spoon, until egg cooks and soup slightly thickens. Do not boil, or eggs will curdle. Add salt and pepper to taste, then sprinkle with dill or parsley. Serve hot or cold.

Makes 4 servings.

64

Broccoli Leek Soup

Chef: Laura Pensiero

Fresh leeks and broccoli—two overlooked vegetables that should be at the top of the charts—come together in a gorgeous, warming soup.

1 large bunch broccoli (about 1½ pounds)
1 Tbsp. olive oil
1 Tbsp. unsalted butter
2 medium leeks, white and light green parts only, thinly sliced
1 medium baking potato, peeled and cut into 1-inch pieces
1 garlic clove, thinly sliced
3 cups low-sodium chicken or vegetable broth
¾ tsp. salt
Pinch of freshly ground pepper
¼ cup half-and-half (optional)
¼ cup snipped chives

1 Separate broccoli stems from florets. Using a vegetable peeler, peel stems to remove tough outer layer, then slice into ¼-inch-thick "coins." Break or cut the florets into small pieces. Reserve stems and florets separately.

2 In a medium saucepan, heat oil and butter over medium heat. Add leeks and cook, stirring often, until softened and fragrant, about 3 minutes. Add broccoli stems, potato, and garlic, and cook 2 to 3 minutes. Add 3 cups water, broth, salt, and pepper; bring to a boil. Reduce heat; cover partially and simmer until broccoli and potato are tender, about 12 minutes.

3 Add florets; bring to a boil and then simmer 5 minutes. Transfer soup in batches to a blender or food processor, and puree until smooth. Return soup to saucepan; add half-and-half (if using) and chives, and reheat briefly.

Makes 4 servings.

Creole Gumbo

Chef: Leah Chase

Have a taste of traditional Big Easy cooking with this rich and flavor-intense stew packed with oysters, crab, chicken, shrimp, and sausage.

4 live hard-shell crabs, cleaned*

1 pound boneless, skinless chicken thighs, cut into 1-inch pieces

½ pound andouille sausage, cut into bite-size pieces

½ pound kielbasa, cut into bite-size pieces

½ pound veal stew meat

¼ cup vegetable oil

¼ cup all-purpose flour

1 medium onion, chopped

6 chicken wings, tips removed, cut in half at joint

½ pound smoked ham, diced

1 Tbsp. paprika

¼ cup chopped flat-leaf parsley

3 large garlic cloves, minced

1 tsp. ground thyme

1 tsp. salt

1 pound medium shrimp, peeled and deveined

24 shucked oysters (½ pint) with their liquid (optional)

1 Tbsp. filé powder**

5 cups hot cooked rice, to serve

*If live crabs aren't available, substitute 4 ounces fresh crabmeat. **For filé powder, visit www.cajungrocer.com.

1 In an 8-quart Dutch oven, combine crabs (if using crabmeat, add in fourth step with shrimp and oysters), chicken thighs, both sausages, and veal. Cover and cook over medium heat for 30 minutes, stirring occasionally.

2 Heat oil in a medium-size skillet over medium heat. Add flour and cook, stirring constantly, until mixture (called a roux) turns the color of pecans, about 5 minutes. Reduce heat to low and add onion. Cook, stirring constantly, until onion softens, about 3 minutes.

3 Stir roux into pot with crab mixture. Gradually add 3 quarts of water, stirring to combine and scraping any brown bits from bottom and sides of pot. Bring to a boil. Stir in chicken wings, ham, paprika, parsley, garlic, thyme, and salt. Return to a boil, then reduce heat; simmer 1 hour, stirring occasionally.

4 Add shrimp and oysters (if using); simmer 10 minutes. Remove pot from heat and stir in filé powder. Let stand 5 minutes. Serve over rice.

Makes 8 to 10 servings.

Deep, dusky gumbo is the world's best medicine when New Orleans people feel homesick, says Leah Chase. "Around here, we can go a mile on a bowl of it."

Curried Cauliflower & Apple Soup with Cilantro Cream

Chef: Daniel Boulud

A rich soup with a gloriously distinct flavor, this is a meal in itself. The cilantro cream is a lovely touch.

3 Tbsp. unsalted butter

2 medium onions, peeled and finely diced

4 tsp. Madras (hot) curry powder, divided

Pinch of saffron

4 Golden Delicious apples

½ tsp. freshly ground white pepper

Salt and additional pepper to taste

2½ medium heads cauliflower, broken into small florets (about 14 cups)

2 fresh thyme sprigs

1 bay leaf

10 cups unsalted chicken stock or low-sodium canned broth

2 cups heavy cream

2 Tbsp. finely chopped cilantro leaves, plus more for garnish

18 medium shrimp, cooked, peeled, deveined, and halved (optional)

1 Heat butter in large, heavy saucepan over medium heat. Add onions, 3½ tsp. curry powder, and saffron, stirring until onions start to soften, 5 to 7 minutes.

2 Peel, core, and thinly slice 3 apples. Add apple slices, ½ tsp. white pepper, and salt to taste and continue to cook, stirring, for 5 minutes.

3 Add cauliflower, thyme, bay leaf, and chicken stock and bring to a boil. Reduce heat and simmer 20 to 25 minutes—skimming the surface regularly to remove any fat and foam—until cauliflower is tender when pierced with a knife.

4 Add 1¼ cups of cream and boil 2 minutes. Remove from heat; discard bay leaf and thyme sprigs.

5 Transfer soup in batches to a blender or food processor, and puree until very smooth. For the smoothest consistency, strain the soup through a fine-mesh sieve. Taste, and adjust seasoning if necessary.

6 Just before serving the soup, peel, core, and finely dice the remaining apple. Toss apple with remaining ½ tsp. curry powder, and add salt and pepper to taste. Place in a small saucepan with 1 Tbsp. water. Cover and cook over medium to low heat for 3 to 4 minutes, or until apple is tender.

7 Whip remaining cream until soft peaks form. Season with salt and pepper to taste and fold in cilantro.

8 Ladle soup into bowls. Top with a little of the diced-apple mixture, a spoonful of cilantro cream, several fresh cilantro leaves, and 2 to 3 shrimp halves, if desired.

Makes 10 to 12 servings.

69

Spiced Butternut Squash & Apple Soup with Maple Pumpernickel Croutons

Chef: Rori Trovato

Butternut squash soup is a quintessential fall dish;
the slightly sweet croutons add a little crunch.

SOUP

2 Tbsp. olive oil

1 medium onion, cut into ½-inch chunks

2 celery stalks, cut into 2 pieces

1 butternut squash (about 3½ pounds), peeled, seeded, and cut into ½-inch chunks

6 cups vegetable or chicken stock

2 tsp. fennel seeds

½ tsp. cinnamon

½ tsp. ground cardamom

1 bay leaf

3 McIntosh apples, peeled, cored, and cut into ½-inch chunks

2 Tbsp. apple cider vinegar

Kosher salt and freshly ground pepper

½ cup plain yogurt, for garnish

CROUTONS

3 Tbsp. olive oil

1 Tbsp. maple syrup

3 Tbsp. finely minced chives

1 tsp. salt

½ tsp. freshly ground pepper

1 small loaf pumpernickel bread, cut into ½-inch chunks

1 To make soup: In a large pot, heat olive oil over medium-high heat. Add onion and celery and cook, stirring, until tender and lightly browned, about 7 minutes. Add squash and cook an additional 3 minutes. Add stock, fennel seeds, cinnamon, cardamom, and bay leaf. Bring to a boil, then reduce to a simmer; cook 15 minutes. Add apples and vinegar and continue cooking 12 minutes. Remove from heat and puree either in batches in a food processor or blender or all together with an emulsion blender. Season with salt and pepper.

2 To make croutons: Preheat oven to 375°. In a large bowl, combine olive oil, maple syrup, chives, salt, and pepper. Add bread and toss well. On a baking sheet, spread croutons in a single layer and bake until golden brown and crispy, 7 to 12 minutes, using a spatula to turn once or twice. Remove from oven and cool. Garnish soup with yogurt and croutons.

Makes 6 servings.

Thai Chicken Coconut Curry Soup

Chef: Rori Trovato

Slightly exotic and completely delicious, this chicken soup needs no accompaniments.
If you like coconut and curry, you'll be in paradise.

4 cups chicken stock

5 garlic cloves, peeled and cut into
large chunks

2 inches fresh ginger, peeled and cut
into large chunks

1 Tbsp. Thai green curry paste

2 tsp. whole coriander seeds

1 tsp. whole cumin seeds

½ tsp. whole black peppercorns

¾ cup loosely packed cilantro leaves
and stems, plus additional ½ cup,
chopped, for garnish

1 cup unsweetened coconut milk

¾ cup thinly sliced shallots

1 cup sliced mushrooms

One (4- to 6-ounce) boneless chicken
breast, cut into ¼-inch strips

2 Tbsp. Asian fish sauce (nam pla)

2 Tbsp. fresh lime juice

2 tsp. brown sugar

1 jalapeño, sliced into rings (optional)

1 small tomato, seeded and diced, for
garnish

½ cup freshly shaved coconut or
unsweetened coconut flakes,
toasted, for garnish

1 In a large heavy-bottomed pot over high heat, combine chicken stock, garlic, ginger, curry paste, coriander, cumin, peppercorns, and cilantro. Bring to a boil; reduce heat and simmer 30 minutes. Strain broth through a fine-mesh sieve over a bowl; discard solids. Return broth to pot; add coconut milk, shallots, mushrooms, and chicken. Return to a boil, then reduce heat to a simmer and cook until chicken is cooked through, 5 to 7 minutes.

2 In a small bowl, combine fish sauce, lime juice, brown sugar, and jalapeño, if desired; stir until sugar is dissolved, then add mixture to soup. Garnish with tomato, coconut flakes, and cilantro; serve hot.

Makes 4 servings.

Callaloo

Chef: Marcus Samuelsson

This classic Caribbean soup gets its emerald color from chopped spinach.

2 Tbsp. peanut oil

1 medium Spanish onion, chopped

2 garlic cloves, minced

2 bird's-eye chilies, seeds and ribs
 removed, finely chopped*

1 ½ tsp. ground cumin

1 ½ tsp. coriander seeds, crushed

2 cups chicken stock or broth

1 cup coconut milk

1 cup bottled clam juice

1 cup heavy cream

Two (10-ounce) packages frozen
 chopped spinach, thawed

Juice of 2 to 3 limes (about ¼ cup),
 plus more to taste

½ tsp. salt

*If you can't find bird's-eye chilies, use
¼ tsp. crushed red pepper flakes.

1 Heat oil in a Dutch oven over medium-high heat. When oil is so hot it simmers, add onion, garlic, and chilies. Sauté until onion is translucent, about 3 minutes.

2 Add cumin, coriander, chicken stock, coconut milk, clam juice, and heavy cream; bring to a gentle simmer. Cook, partially covered, 30 minutes.

3 Add spinach and bring to a boil. Reduce heat and simmer, stirring occasionally, until spinach is cooked, about 5 minutes.

4 In a blender, puree soup in batches until smooth. Transfer to bowls. Stir in lime juice and salt to taste. Serve hot.

Makes 4 servings.

74

Tomato & Cucumber Sandwiches with Herbed Feta Butter

Created by Susan Quick

For unexpected flair and flavor, make this classic tea sandwich with herbed feta butter.

½ small red onion, thinly sliced

4 ounces (reduced-fat) Neufchâtel cream cheese, room temperature

4 Tbsp. butter, room temperature

⅓ cup crumbled feta cheese

2 Tbsp. minced fresh mint leaves

2 Tbsp. minced fresh chives

16 slices very thin white or wheat bread

2 very ripe plum tomatoes, seeded and chopped

½ medium English (seedless) cucumber, peeled and thinly sliced

Salt to taste

1 cup radish, garlic, or other spicy sprouts

1 Rinse onion slices beneath cold running water for 30 seconds (to remove sharp onion flavor); drain, pat dry with paper towels, and set aside.

2 Combine cream cheese, butter, feta, mint, and chives in a bowl; set aside.

3 Using a 2½-inch round biscuit cutter, cut bread slices into rounds. Spread cheese mixture on bread rounds. Place chopped tomatoes on 8 bread rounds. Arrange 2 to 3 overlapping cucumber slices on remaining bread rounds. Sprinkle with salt. Top sandwiches with a small amount of sliced onion and sprouts. Arrange on serving platter.

Makes 16 sandwiches.

Top: **Tomato & Cucumber Sandwiches;** Middle: **Chutney Chicken Salad Tea Sandwiches** (recipe on page 81) Bottom: **Ham, Pepper-Cheese, & Apple Tea Sandwiches** (recipe on page 79)

Curried Chicken Sandwich

Chef: Margaux Sky

Curry and chicken love each other, as is obvious
with one bite of this sandwich.

20 whole black peppercorns

2 bay leaves

2 whole cloves

½ lemon

3 pounds medium chicken tenders

½ cup plus 2 Tbsp. spicy brown
  mustard

½ cup honey

1 ¼ tsp. curry powder

¾ tsp. lemon pepper

⅛ tsp. salt

Butter, for spreading

1 loaf challah or other rich egg bread,
  cut into 12 thick slices

½ cup shredded carrots

½ cup slivered almonds

2 medium tomatoes, chopped

1 bag (about 5 ounces) mesclun salad
  greens

Red grapes and assorted berries for
  garnish

1 In a large saucepan over high heat, combine peppercorns, bay leaves, cloves, lemon, and 14 cups water; cover and bring to a boil. Add chicken and cook, uncovered, stirring occasionally, 7 to 10 minutes, or until cooked through; drain. Once cool, quarter each tender crosswise.

2 In a large bowl, combine mustard, honey, curry powder, lemon pepper, and salt; stir in chicken. Cover and refrigerate at least 30 minutes or up to 1 day.

3 Butter both sides of bread slices. In a heated nonstick skillet over medium-high heat, cook bread in batches 3 to 5 minutes, or until browned, turning once.

4 Combine carrots and almonds with chicken mixture. Divide chicken curry among 6 bread slices. Top with tomatoes, mesclun, and remaining bread slices. Serve with fruit.

Makes 6 servings.

Ham, Pepper-Cheese, & Apple Tea Sandwiches

Created by Susan Quick

What a delectable sandwich to serve alongside tea! The raisin bread adds a note of sweetness to offset the creamy Boursin cheese and paper-thin slices of ham.

8 slices raisin bread
1 package (5.2 ounces) Boursin pepper-cheese spread, room temperature
½ pound thinly sliced baked ham
½ bunch arugula leaves, stems removed, rinsed well and spun dry
1 Granny Smith apple
2 Tbsp. fresh lemon juice

1 Spread bread slices generously with pepper-cheese spread. Top with 2 folded slices of ham. Use a serrated knife to trim crusts into rectangles, approximately 2½" x 3".

2 Tuck 2 to 3 arugula leaves between ham slices.

3 Thinly slice apple and dip in lemon juice to keep slices from turning brown. Arrange 3 slices on top of each sandwich. (Sandwiches can be made up to an hour ahead. Cover with damp paper towels and wrap tightly with plastic wrap. Refrigerate until ready to serve.)

Makes 8 sandwiches.

Tomato Sandwich

Created by Celia Barbour

A perfectly ripe tomato is the most important ingredient here. It should be summertime juicy and grown close by; otherwise there's not much point to the sandwich!

1 ripe tomato
2 slices bread, preferably white farm or peasant
1 Tbsp. mayonnaise
Salt and pepper (optional)

Slice the tomato thickly—about as thick as a slice of bread. Spread the bread with mayonnaise. Place the tomato on one slice. Sprinkle with salt and a little pepper, if you like. Top with the other slice of bread. Cut the sandwich in half. Go outside.

Makes 1 sandwich.

At the Table with Leah Chase
REVIVING THE SOUL OF NEW ORLEANS, ONE DISH AT A TIME

"If you go into any home in New Orleans, you will find a good cook," Leah Chase says of her beloved city. As everyone knows, food is a significant part of the culture in the Crescent City, but perhaps no one knows this as deeply as Leah.

Not only is she one of the leading culinary lights of the The Big Easy; she is a national treasure as well. Leah has cooked at Dooky Chase Restaurant—located at 2301 Orleans Street—since almost forever. The restaurant, named for her husband, belonged to his parents when Leah married into the family in the 1940s. She started working there and by the middle of the 1950s, she took over the kitchen, turning out some of the best Creole food anywhere in a city of superlatives.

The restaurant was one of the first where African Americans were invited to sit down and eat a meal, and it soon became a popular meeting place. During the 1960s, leaders of the Civil Rights Movement could be found enjoying Leah's gumbo and stuffed shrimp, and during the next decades, the restaurant's reputation flowered so that before long, Leah, dubbed the "Queen of Creole Cooking," had won every award a restaurateur and chef could win. She is the author of two books: *And I Still Cook* and *The Dooky Chase Cookbook*.

And then came Hurricane Katrina. The monumental storm destroyed the restaurant and caused Leah and her family to flee their city. "I spent about a week and a half in Birmingham," she recalls of those harrowing days. "And then I was in Baton Rouge for two or three months." As soon as she was able, she returned to New Orleans and lived in a FEMA trailer until she and her husband could move into a house near the restaurant. Meanwhile, her grandsons worked tirelessly to clean out the building so that the family could rebuild Dooky Chase.

Leah can't believe how long the rebuilding took and how difficult it was, but she is grateful for all the help she got from her family, the community, and her customers. Louisiana chef John Folse was instrumental in

> "We stuff everything. Shrimp, peppers, crab—you name it!"

getting her up and running, she says, and she is also beholden to Southbend Ranges. The CEO hauled away her old, hurricane-battered stove for the company's museum and donated a brand new one. "I just love cooking on it," she says today. And the stove gets a workout since Leah, despite her 85 years, cooks all the food for the restaurant.

"It's been hard for the locals not to have the food they like," she says. When she reopened her take-out business in September 2007, about a month before the restaurant opened, customers flocked to buy gumbo, oyster sandwiches, and fried oysters. "Stewed chicken with brown gravy and baked macaroni and cheese has been in great demand," she says. "I am not sure why but I think this kind of food makes people feel good."

No wonder: Good Creole cuisine can't be beat. Its melange of seasonings and spices and reliance on fresh-as-can-be ingredients blend superbly. "We stuff everything," Leah says, laughing. "Shrimp, peppers, crab—you name it."

Although the restaurant was not quite ready for customers when President George W. Bush requested a meal at Dooky Chase's on August 28, 2007, Leah obliged. "It's the first time a president has visited this area," she says, referring to the historic Treme district, the South's oldest settlement of free slaves of color. Hosting the Bushes was "quite an experience," she says: Both the President and First Lady were very gracious and stayed for a "good long dinner of gumbo, fish, sorbet, and dessert."

New Orleans is still on a long road to recovery. Preserving the indigenous food and distinct culture is integral to restoring the spirit of the city. Leah Chase is on a mission to revive the soul of the city, with every dish she serves.

Leah Chase's Recipe
■ Creole Gumbo (page 68)

Chutney Chicken Salad Tea Sandwiches

Created by Susan Quick

The mango gives this salad a tantalizing touch of sweetness.

1 pound boneless, skinless chicken breasts
Salt and freshly ground pepper to taste
½ cup finely diced celery
3 Tbsp. finely diced red onion
4 Tbsp. finely chopped flat-leaf parsley
1 cup walnuts, toasted and chopped
⅓ cup mayonnaise
1 Tbsp. fresh lemon juice
3 Tbsp. Major Grey's (mango-ginger) Chutney
16 slices very thin white bread
4 Tbsp. butter, room temperature

1 In a large pot of boiling salted water, simmer chicken 15 to 20 minutes, or just until cooked through. Drain and transfer to a plate to cool 10 minutes.

2 Thinly slice chicken into strips, then finely chop. Season with salt and pepper.

3 Toss chicken with celery, onion, parsley, and walnuts. In another bowl, stir together mayonnaise, lemon juice, and chutney. Add to chicken mixture and blend well. Taste and adjust seasonings, if necessary.

4 Place approximately ½ cup chicken salad on each of 8 slices of bread; spread and press salad onto bread to make an even layer. Butter remaining 8 slices and place on top of chicken salad. Trim crusts to make even squares. Slice sandwiches in half to form 16 triangles. (Sandwiches may be made to this point up to an hour ahead. Cover with damp paper towels and wrap tightly with plastic wrap. Refrigerate until ready to serve.) Arrange on serving platter.

Makes 16 sandwiches.

81

Egg Salad with Tarragon Mustard

Chef: Paula Disbrowe

Whether it's in beef stew or egg salad, mustard has that extra bite, a sharpness. And it cuts the richness.

6 large eggs
⅓ cup mayonnaise
2 tsp. tarragon (or Dijon) mustard
¼ tsp. salt
⅛ tsp. freshly ground pepper
1 small shallot, finely chopped
1 celery stalk, finely chopped
1 Tbsp. capers
1 Tbsp. chopped fresh tarragon
1 Tbsp. chopped fresh cilantro

1 Bring a medium saucepan filled three quarters with water to a boil. Add eggs and cook 9 minutes (center of yolk will be slightly creamy). Carefully pour off hot water and rinse eggs with cold running water to cool. Peel eggs and roughly chop.

2 Meanwhile, in a large bowl, combine mayonnaise, mustard, salt, and pepper. Add remaining ingredients. Gently fold in eggs.

Makes 2½ cups.

82

Buster Crab, Lettuce, & Tomato Po'boy

Chef: John Besh

This po'boy is stuffed with an embarrassment of riches:
soft-shell crab, crisp lettuce, and ripe tomatoes.

3 cups canola oil
1 cup buttermilk
8 small soft-shell crabs, cleaned
1 cup all-purpose flour
½ cup cornmeal
1 tsp. salt
¾ tsp. freshly ground pepper
¼ cup mayonnaise, plus more to taste
1 loaf French bread, cut into 4 equal pieces, halved horizontally and toasted
8 Bibb or Boston lettuce leaves
8 dill pickle slices
2 Creole or beefsteak tomatoes, sliced
Hot sauce to taste

1 In a large, deep sauté pan or skillet over medium-high heat, bring oil to 350° on a deep-fat thermometer.

2 While oil heats, pour buttermilk into a shallow dish. Place crabs in buttermilk; turn to coat, and let stand 5 minutes. On another plate, mix flour, cornmeal, ½ tsp. salt, and ½ tsp. pepper. Season crabs with ¼ tsp. salt and ¼ tsp. pepper, then remove crabs from buttermilk one at a time and coat with flour mixture. Place crabs on a baking sheet.

3 Carefully add crabs, four at a time, to hot oil. Cook until golden, about 1½ minutes per side. With a slotted spoon, transfer crabs to paper towels to drain.

4 Spread mayonnaise on cut sides of bread. Top each bottom half with 2 lettuce leaves, 2 pickle slices, and tomato slices. Sprinkle tomatoes with the remaining ¼ tsp. salt. Top with crabs. Add top halves of bread. Serve with hot sauce.

Makes 4 sandwiches.

84

Chicken & Pancetta Panini with Fontina, Arugula, & Provençal Mustard

Chef: Paula Disbrowe

Balance the decadence of rich pancetta and Fontina cheese with a lean chicken breast in this flavorful hot sandwich.

6 boneless, skinless chicken breast halves
½ tsp. salt
¼ tsp. freshly ground pepper
1 tsp. olive oil, plus additional oil for brushing grill
12 thin slices pancetta
Six (4" x 4") squares focaccia (such as rosemary), split horizontally
2 cups shredded Italian Fontina
1 bunch arugula leaves
6 tsp. Provençal, tarragon, or any herbed mustard

1 Heat a panini grill or grill pan over low heat. Place each chicken breast between two sheets of waxed paper; gently pound with a meat mallet or the bottom of a small, heavy saucepan until evenly thick. Season both sides of chicken with salt and pepper.

2 In a large skillet, heat 1 tsp. olive oil over medium heat. Cook pancetta in batches until golden. Remove each batch with a slotted spoon, and drain on paper towels.

3 Meanwhile, lightly brush grill or grill pan with olive oil. Working in batches, grill chicken, covered, just until cooked through, about 5 minutes.

4 To assemble panini: Place a chicken breast on the bottom half of each square of focaccia. Top with 2 slices pancetta, ⅓ cup Fontina, and 3 or 4 arugula leaves. Spread 1 tsp. mustard on other half of bread and place on top of arugula. With the palm of your hand, press down gently. Repeat with remaining chicken breasts.

5 Place 1 or 2 panini on grill or in pan; cover and cook until cheese melts and bread is toasted, about 5 minutes. Slice each sandwich in half. Repeat with the remaining panini.

Makes 6 servings.

Rib Eye Steaks with Cornmeal-Fried Onion Rings
(recipe on page 92)

Chapter 4

MEAT

Grilled Skirt Steak Salad

Chef: April Bloomfield

Skirt steak is an incredibly tasty cut. When paired with tender greens and a citrus dressing, it becomes a main-course salad.

DRESSING
¼ cup finely chopped shallots
1 Tbsp. freshly grated lime peel
2 Tbsp. fresh lime juice
2 Tbsp. extra-virgin olive oil
1 Tbsp. Dijon mustard
¾ tsp. kosher salt

GARNISH
Peanut oil, for frying
½ cup all-purpose flour
4 medium shallots, thinly sliced, rings separated
3 long hot red chilies, thinly sliced
½ tsp. kosher salt

STEAK AND SALAD
2 pounds skirt steak, cut into 4 pieces, excess fat trimmed, room temperature
1 tsp. kosher salt
2 limes, halved
1 Tbsp. extra-virgin olive oil
3 bunches watercress, trimmed
1 cup fresh chervil leaves
Sea salt

1 To make dressing: In a medium bowl, whisk together shallots, lime peel and juice, olive oil, mustard, and salt. Whisk to combine.

2 To make garnish: In a medium-deep saucepan, heat 1 inch peanut oil to 325°. While oil heats, divide flour between two bowls. Toss shallots in one bowl and chilies in the other. Shake excess flour from shallots and fry in batches until golden and crisp, 3 to 4 minutes. Remove with slotted spoon to paper towel–lined cookie sheet. Repeat with chilies. Sprinkle with salt.

3 To make steak and salad: Preheat a grill or stovetop grill pan to medium-high. Sprinkle steak on both sides with salt. Cook 2 to 3 minutes per side for medium-rare. Remove to a large bowl and squeeze juice from lime halves over steak; drizzle with oil. Let stand while preparing salad.

4 In a large bowl, gently toss watercress, chervil, dressing, and a pinch of crushed sea salt. Remove steak to a cutting board, reserving juices in bowl. Thinly slice steak. Place half of salad on a serving platter. Top with half of sliced steak. Reserve a small amount of salad to garnish top, and repeat with remaining salad and steak. Whisk reserved juices in bowl and add salt to taste. Drizzle juices over salad. Sprinkle with shallots and chilies.

Makes 8 servings.

Barley Risotto with Mushrooms & Tenderloin of Beef

Chef: Cary Neff

The barley-and-wild-mushroom risotto is the star of this dish,
with the beef playing a supporting role.

RISOTTO

4 cups vegetable broth
1 cup pearl barley
¼ tsp. extra-virgin olive oil
¼ cup chopped onion
½ tsp. minced garlic
1 ½ cups (about 2 ounces) assorted
  seasonal fresh mushrooms (shiitake,
  oyster, portobello, chanterelle)
1 bay leaf
½ tsp. chopped fresh thyme
½ tsp. chopped fresh oregano
Pinch of freshly ground pepper
2 Tbsp. Parmigiano-Reggiano cheese,
  optional

RED WINE REDUCTION

2 cups red wine
2 Tbsp. light corn syrup

TENDERLOIN

Four (4-ounce) filets mignons (beef
  tenderloin steaks)
1 Tbsp. finely chopped fresh herbs
  (basil, oregano, parsley, and thyme)
½ tsp. salt
½ tsp. pepper
½ tsp. extra-virgin olive oil

2 cups assorted steamed vegetables

1 To make risotto: In a 2-quart saucepan over high heat, bring broth and 1 cup water to a boil. Then reduce heat to maintain a simmer.

2 In a medium skillet over medium heat, toast ½ cup barley, stirring constantly, until golden brown and fragrant, about 5 minutes. Set aside.

3 In a medium saucepan over medium heat, heat oil. Add onion and garlic; cook, stirring, until onion softens, about 2 minutes. Add mushrooms and cook 2 minutes. Stir in toasted barley, remaining ½ cup barley, and bay leaf. Add about ½ cup simmering broth to barley, stirring until liquid has been absorbed. Continue cooking, adding broth ½ cup at a time and stirring, until all liquid has been absorbed and barley is tender, 30 to 35 minutes. Stir in thyme, oregano, pepper, and cheese. Remove bay leaf.

4 To make wine reduction: In a small saucepan over medium-high heat, bring wine and corn syrup to a boil until reduced to a syrupy consistency, about 20 minutes. Set aside.

5 To make tenderloin: Sprinkle filets with herbs, salt, and pepper. In a large nonstick skillet over medium-high heat, heat oil. Add filets and cook until browned, about 3 minutes on both sides for medium-rare or until desired doneness.

6 To serve: Press ½ cup risotto into a 4-ounce ramekin or custard cup and unmold in center of plate. Repeat to make 3 more molds. Slice each filet horizontally into 4 round medallions. Arrange ½ cup steamed vegetables on each plate. Lean beef slices against risotto. Drizzle 1 Tbsp. wine reduction over beef, risotto, and vegetables.

Makes 4 servings.

Rib Eye Steaks with Cornmeal-Fried Onion Rings

Chef: Ina Garten

Golden onion rings are a crunchy companion to these succulent steaks.

4 (1¼-inch-thick) rib eye steaks, either boneless or bone in
Kosher salt
Freshly ground pepper
Good olive oil

ONION RINGS
2 large Spanish onions (or 3 yellow onions)
2 cups buttermilk
Kosher salt
Freshly ground black pepper
1 ½ cups all-purpose flour
¼ cup (medium) yellow cornmeal
1 quart vegetable oil

*For 1½-inch steaks, sear them for 2 minutes on each side and then cook them for 4 to 6 minutes, until the internal temperature reaches 120°. Allow to rest before serving.

1 Thirty minutes before grilling the steaks, remove them from the refrigerator and allow them to come to room temperature. Heat a grill with coals, preferably using a charcoal chimney.

2 When the coals are hot, spread them out in the grill in one solid layer. Pat the steaks dry on both sides with paper towels and sprinkle them liberally with salt and pepper. Place the steaks on the hot grill and sear them on each side for 2 minutes, until browned. Brush each side lightly with olive oil. Place the lid on the grill and allow the steaks to cook for another 3 to 4 minutes, until they are cooked rare, or 120° on a meat thermometer.* (To test the steaks, insert the thermometer sideways to be sure you're actually testing the middle of the steak.) Remove steaks from the grill, place them in one layer on a platter, and cover tightly with aluminum foil. Allow the steaks to rest at room temperature for 15 minutes. Slice and serve warm with cornmeal-fried onion rings.

3 To make onion rings: Peel the onions, then slice them ½ to ¾ inch thick and separate them into rings. Combine the buttermilk, 1 ½ teaspoons salt, and 1 teaspoon pepper in a medium bowl. Add the onion rings, toss well, and allow to marinate for at least 15 minutes. (The onion rings can sit in the buttermilk for a few hours.) In a separate bowl, combine the flour, cornmeal, 1 teaspoon salt, and ½ teaspoon pepper. Set aside.

4 When you're ready to fry the onion rings, preheat the oven to 200°. Line a baking sheet with paper towels. Heat the oil to 350° in a large pot or Dutch oven. (A candy thermometer attached to the side of the pot will help you maintain the proper temperature.) Working in batches, lift some onions out of the buttermilk and dredge them in the flour mixture. Drop into the hot oil and fry for 2 minutes, until golden brown, turning them once with tongs. Don't crowd them! Place the finished onion rings on the baking sheet, sprinkle liberally with salt, and keep them warm in the oven while you fry the next batches. Continue to fry the onion rings and place them in the warm oven until all the onions are fried. They will remain crisp in the oven for up to 30 minutes. Serve hot.

Serves 4 to 6.

Grilled Tenderloin of Beef with Spicy Fresh Herb Vinaigrette

Chef: Rori Trovato

This robust and juicy dish is even better the next day. Serve any leftover sliced steak in a sandwich, or try the marinade as a fresh pasta sauce.

VINAIGRETTE

1 cup parsley leaves, loosely packed

1 cup basil leaves, loosely packed

½ cup mint leaves, loosely packed

1 Tbsp. fresh thyme leaves

¼ tsp. red pepper flakes, or more to taste

1 large clove garlic

2 Tbsp. white wine vinegar

⅔ cup olive oil

1 tsp. kosher salt, plus more to taste

BEEF

1 tenderloin of beef, trimmed (about 5 to 6 pounds)

2 Tbsp. olive oil

2 tsp. kosher salt

2 tsp. cracked black pepper

1 To make vinaigrette: In a blender or the bowl of a food processor fitted with knife blade, combine herbs, red pepper flakes, and garlic. Pulse until well chopped. Add vinegar and pulse to combine. With the motor running, slowly add ⅔ cup olive oil until vinaigrette is almost pureed. Add salt and adjust seasoning to taste. Transfer to a serving bowl and set aside.

2 To make beef: Preheat gas grill to medium-high, or prepare a charcoal grill for direct grilling over medium-high heat. Brush meat with olive oil and sprinkle with salt and pepper. Place on grill, cover, and cook 30 to 40 minutes, turning every 5 minutes. For rare beef, remove from grill when a meat thermometer reads 115° (120° for medium rare). Let sit 20 minutes; the temperature of the tenderloin will rise about 10 degrees and it will continue to cook. Slice and serve warm or at room temperature, topped with herb vinaigrette.

Makes 8 to 10 servings.

The vinaigrette can be prepared several hours in advance of the beef.

93

Beef Stew with Cognac & Horseradish Mustard

Chef: Paula Disbrowe

Few dishes make us feel as comforted as an old-fashioned beef stew. The splash of Cognac just makes it better.

About 3 Tbsp. olive oil

¼ pound applewood-smoked bacon, cut into ½-inch pieces

2 large sweet onions, chopped

2 shallots, chopped

2 garlic cloves, minced

3 Tbsp. all-purpose flour

Salt and freshly ground pepper

2 pounds beef chuck, cut into 2-inch cubes

½ cup Cognac

3 cups beef broth

1 cup chopped canned Italian plum tomatoes

2 fresh bay leaves, torn, or 1 dried bay leaf

4 thyme branches, lightly crushed

⅓ cup horseradish (or Dijon) mustard

2 large carrots, cut into 1-inch pieces

2 large parsnips, cut into 1-inch pieces

½ pound cremini mushrooms, sliced

¼ cup red wine

1 In a large Dutch oven, heat 1 Tbsp. olive oil over medium-low heat. Add bacon and cook until crisp. Remove with a slotted spoon and drain on paper towels. Increase heat to medium-high. Add onions and shallots and cook until they begin to turn golden (but not brown), about 15 minutes. Add garlic and cook 1 minute. Using a slotted spoon, transfer mixture to a large bowl.

2 In another large bowl, combine flour, 1 tsp. salt, and ¼ tsp. pepper. Add beef and toss with seasoned flour. In the Dutch oven over medium-high heat, cook one third of beef until browned on all sides, about 5 minutes. Add beef to the bowl of onions. Repeat with remaining beef in two more batches, adding another Tbsp. olive oil as necessary.

3 Add Cognac to pot, scraping up any browned bits from the bottom. Stir in broth, tomatoes, bay leaves, thyme, and mustard until well combined. Return meat-and-onion mixture and bacon to pot. Reduce heat and simmer, partially covered, until meat is soft, about 2 hours. Add carrots and parsnips; cover and simmer until tender, about 45 minutes.

4 Meanwhile, in a large skillet, heat 1 Tbsp. olive oil over medium-high heat. Add mushrooms and cook until browned.

5 Stir mushrooms and wine into stew; simmer 10 minutes. Season to taste with salt and pepper. Remove bay leaves and thyme branches. Serve with a simple green salad.

Makes 6 servings.

Ropa Vieja

Created by Andrew Friedman

Ropa vieja means "old clothes" but is actually a mighty tasty, slow-simmered, steak–and–bell pepper stew.

Two (1½-pound) flank steaks, trimmed of excess fat and cut crosswise into 3 pieces each
Kosher salt and freshly ground black pepper
7 Tbsp. canola or vegetable oil
3 large Spanish onions, 1 quartered and 2 thinly sliced
1 green bell pepper, cored, seeded, and thinly sliced
1 yellow bell pepper, cored, seeded, and thinly sliced
4 cups low-sodium chicken broth
2 bay leaves
1 Tbsp. whole black peppercorns
1 tsp. ground cumin
1 red bell pepper, cored, seeded, and thinly sliced
4 large garlic cloves, thinly sliced
1 Tbsp. tomato paste
One (14½-ounce) can whole tomatoes in juice, crushed with fingers
½ cup sliced Spanish olives

1 Season flank steak with ½ tsp. salt and ½ tsp. pepper.

2 In a heavy-bottomed 5- to 6-quart pot, heat 2 Tbsp. oil over medium-high heat. Add half of sliced steak to pot in a single layer and cook until well browned, about 2 minutes per side. Transfer steak to a plate. Pour off any oil in pot and repeat with 2 Tbsp. oil and remaining steak.

3 In the same pot, heat 1 Tbsp. oil over medium-high heat. Add quartered onion, half of green pepper, and half of yellow pepper. Cook, stirring frequently, until vegetables are lightly browned, about 5 minutes.

4 Add chicken broth, bay leaves, peppercorns, cumin, and ½ tsp. salt. Add cooked steak and any juices on the plate. The steak should be just covered with broth; pour in additional broth, if necessary. Bring to a boil; reduce heat to low and simmer, covered, until steak is fork-tender, 2¼ to 2½ hours. Remove pot from heat and let steak cool in broth for 30 minutes.

5 Transfer steak to a plate. Strain cooking liquid through a sieve set over a bowl; discard solids. Let liquid stand 5 minutes, then skim off and discard any fat. Set cooking liquid aside. Shred steak.

6 In the same pot, heat 2 Tbsp. oil over medium heat. Add thinly sliced onions, remaining green and yellow peppers, red pepper, garlic, ½ tsp. salt, and ¼ tsp. pepper. Cook, stirring frequently, until onions and peppers soften, 15 to 20 minutes.

7 Stir in tomato paste until vegetables are coated. Stir in crushed tomatoes with their juice, 2½ cups of the reserved cooking liquid, and ¼ tsp. salt. Bring to a boil; reduce heat to low and simmer until slightly thickened, about 20 minutes.

8 Return shredded steak to stew and cook until heated through, stirring occasionally, about 2 minutes. Stir in olives. Taste and adjust seasoning with additional salt and pepper if necessary. If not serving immediately, cool, cover, and refrigerate for up to 2 days; flavor will only improve upon standing. Serve with black beans and white rice, boiled potatoes, or fried plantains.

Makes 8 servings.

Orange-Ginger Pork Medallions

Chef: Laura Pensiero

Pork loves the sweet-and-sour flavors of orange juice and fresh ginger. You will, too.

1 cup fresh orange juice

1 tsp. cornstarch

2 Tbsp. peanut oil

¼ cup finely chopped shallots

2 Tbsp. minced peeled fresh ginger

2 garlic cloves, minced

¼ tsp. red pepper flakes

½ cup chicken broth

1 Tbsp. soy sauce

Two (1-pound) pork tenderloins,
  each cut crosswise into 6 slices

½ tsp. salt

¼ tsp. freshly ground pepper

1 Tbsp. unsalted butter

1 In a small bowl, stir together 2 Tbsp. orange juice and corn-starch until smooth. Set aside.

2 In a medium saucepan over medium-high heat, heat 1 Tbsp. oil. Add shallots, ginger, garlic, and red pepper flakes; cook, stirring frequently, until shallots are light golden, about 3 minutes. Add remaining orange juice, broth, and soy sauce. Bring to a boil; boil until reduced to 1 cup, about 6 minutes. Whisk in corn-starch mixture; boil 1 minute. Remove saucepan from heat and set aside.

3 Place pork slices cut side down on work surface and flat-ten slightly with the palm of your hand to make medallions. Sprinkle with salt and pepper.

4 In a 12-inch nonstick skillet over medium-high heat, melt butter with remaining 1 Tbsp. oil. Add pork and cook in batches until browned and cooked through, 4 to 5 minutes per side. Transfer pork to a platter.

5 Add sauce to skillet with drippings; place skillet over medium-high heat. Bring sauce to a boil, stirring to scrape up any brown bits. Stir in juices from pork on platter. Remove skillet from heat and add pork slices to skillet, turning to coat with sauce.

Makes 6 servings.

Cuban 24-Hour Roast Pork

Chef: Alison Mesrop

Sure, it takes time to marinate, but after a day, you're rewarded
with a pork roast that is simply magnificent.

BRINE

½ cup fresh orange or tangerine juice
¼ cup kosher salt
2 Tbsp. packed brown sugar
1 Tbsp. dried rosemary
1 ½ tsp. smoked or sweet paprika
1 ½ tsp. whole black peppercorns
½ tsp. dried oregano
3 garlic cloves, coarsely chopped

One (5- to 6-pound) boneless pork
shoulder roast, tied

GLAZE

½ cup lemon, orange, or tangerine
sorbet
2 Tbsp. fresh tangerine or lemon juice
2 Tbsp. packed brown sugar
1 Tbsp. fresh lime juice

Orange slices, for garnish (optional)
Chopped cilantro, for garnish (optional)
24 Boston lettuce leaves (about 2
heads), for serving
Fresh salsa, for serving

1 To make brine: In a small saucepan, combine orange juice, salt, brown sugar, rosemary, paprika, peppercorns, oregano, and garlic. Bring to a boil; cook, stirring, until salt and sugar dissolve, about 30 seconds. Pour into a large bowl and let cool slightly. Stir in 3½ cups water. Refrigerate until cold, about 30 minutes. Place pork roast in a large Ziploc bag. Pour brine over roast and seal bag. Place bag in a large bowl and refrigerate 24 hours, turning bag once.

2 Preheat oven to 300°. Remove pork from brine and transfer to a large roasting pan. Cover loosely with foil. Roast pork 6 hours, or until meat is very tender.

3 Remove pork from pan and set aside 30 minutes. Pour pan juices into a bowl and skim off fat (or refrigerate until fat hardens, then remove fat and discard). Set aside; do not clean pan.

4 Preheat broiler. Remove strings from pork and return pork to pan.

5 To make glaze: In a bowl, stir together sorbet, tangerine juice, brown sugar, and lime juice. Spread pork with glaze and broil about 5 inches from heat until browned, about 3 minutes. Remove roast to a cutting board and let rest 15 minutes. Add pan juices to other reserved juices and reheat in a saucepan.

6 Thinly slice pork roast and arrange on a platter. Drizzle with some of the hot pan juices; garnish with orange slices and chopped cilantro, if desired. To serve, place a slice or two of pork on a lettuce leaf, top with salsa, roll up, and eat.

*Makes about 12 servings,
with leftovers.*

Lemon Pepper Dry-Rub Ribs with Garden Vegetable Barbecue Sauce

Chef: Michel Nischan

Grilled ribs are reason enough for a party—get ready for sticky fingers and good eats.

SAUCE

1 large head garlic
1 tsp. extra-virgin olive oil
1 Tbsp. grapeseed oil
1 small fennel bulb, trimmed and coarsely chopped
1 small Vidalia onion, coarsely chopped
1 small eggplant, grilled until soft, skin removed
½ cup balsamic vinegar
18 ounces your favorite barbecue sauce
½ cup chopped fresh basil
¼ to ½ cup fresh lemon juice

RIBS

3 (about 1 pound each) racks baby back pork ribs
½ tsp. salt
One (14-ounce) can reduced-sodium chicken broth
2 slices bacon, coarsely chopped
⅓ cup finely grated lemon zest
1 to 2 Tbsp. coarsely ground pepper
2 Tbsp. minced garlic
¼ cup chopped flat-leaf parsley

1 To make sauce: Preheat oven to 425°. Remove papery skin from garlic, leaving bulb intact. Cut thin slice off top to just expose cloves. Drizzle with olive oil and wrap loosely in heavy-duty foil. Bake 45 to 55 minutes, or until cloves are soft; cool. Squeeze pulp from 4 cloves, then set aside.

2 In a large skillet, heat grapeseed oil over medium-high heat. Add fennel and sauté until lightly browned, about 3 minutes. Reduce heat slightly, add onion, and sauté until vegetables are well browned, about 5 minutes. Stir in eggplant, roasted garlic, and vinegar. Cook, stirring to break up eggplant, about 1 minute. Stir in barbecue sauce; reduce heat and simmer 5 minutes to blend flavors. Stir in basil and lemon juice to taste; set aside.

3 To make ribs: Preheat charcoal or gas grill. Remove thin layer of skin from underside of ribs by pulling it off in a sheet. Sprinkle ribs with salt.

4 Place ribs on grill rack. Cover and cook over medium heat 1 hour, turning once.

5 Meanwhile, in a medium saucepan, bring chicken broth and bacon to a boil. Then lower heat and simmer until reduced to ½ cup, about 20 minutes. Set aside to cool.

6 After 1 hour, if using a charcoal grill, add fresh coals to maintain heat. Place ribs over hot part of grill; brush with broth mixture, and sprinkle with some lemon zest and pepper. Cook ribs until browned and tender, about 30 minutes, repeatedly brushing and sprinkling, while turning frequently. Coat ribs with broth once more, then sprinkle with garlic and parsley. Cook, turning frequently, until garlic is golden but not burned, about 10 minutes. Serve with barbecue sauce.

Makes 6 servings.

Moroccan Cinnamon-Rubbed Leg of Lamb

Chef: Rori Trovato

The flavors of North Africa are immediately evoked with cinnamon, cumin, and a taste of honey.

One (4½-pound) semiboneless leg of lamb, trimmed of excess fat
2 Tbsp. honey
2 tsp. ground cumin
1½ tsp. ground black pepper
1 Tbsp. ground cinnamon
2 tsp. kosher salt

1 Preheat oven to 400°. Place a rack on the bottom of a roasting pan large enough to fit lamb.

2 Rinse lamb and pat dry. Rub honey over entire surface, then combine spices and salt and pat into honey Let sit at room temperature 30 minutes.

3 Roast 1 hour and 15 minutes, or until medium-rare (internal temperature should be around 135°; for medium-well, temperature should be 145°). Remove from oven and allow to sit 15 minutes before slicing. Serve with couscous.

Makes 4 servings.

Grilled Lamb with Salsa Verde

Chef: Suzanne Goin

Chunks of tender lamb grilled on skewers taste fantastic with a zesty salsa verde.

4 garlic cloves

2 ½ pounds boneless leg of lamb, cut into 2-inch chunks

2 Tbsp. chopped fresh rosemary

¼ cup plus 3 Tbsp. extra-virgin olive oil

2 tsp. fresh thyme leaves

2 ¼ tsp. cracked black pepper

¾ cup finely chopped, tightly packed flat-leaf parsley leaves

¼ cup finely chopped mint leaves

3 ounces feta cheese, crumbled

6 tsp. fresh lemon juice

1 Tbsp. chopped capers

1 anchovy fillet, mashed

1 tsp. fresh marjoram or oregano leaves

¾ tsp. salt

¼ tsp. freshly ground pepper

6 rosemary branches, leaves removed, or metal skewers

1 head radicchio, leaves separated and torn into large pieces

1 Press 3½ garlic cloves in a garlic press. In a large bowl, combine pressed garlic, lamb, rosemary, 1 Tbsp. olive oil, thyme, and cracked pepper. Cover with plastic wrap and marinate in the refrigerator at least 4 hours or overnight.

2 To make salsa verde: Press remaining ½ garlic clove in garlic press. In a medium bowl, combine pressed garlic, ¼ cup olive oil, parsley, mint, feta, 4 tsp. lemon juice, capers, anchovy, marjoram, ⅛ tsp. salt, and ⅛ tsp. pepper.

3 Prepare grill. Skewer lamb on rosemary branches or metal skewers; sprinkle with ½ tsp. salt. Grill lamb 10 to 12 minutes for medium-rare, or until desired doneness.

4 Meanwhile, in a large bowl, toss radicchio with remaining 2 Tbsp. olive oil, 2 tsp. lemon juice, ⅛ tsp. salt, and ⅛ tsp. pepper; scatter over a platter.

5 Place lamb over radicchio, and spoon salsa verde over top.

Makes 6 servings.

At the Table with Michel Nischan
A MAN ON A MISSION

"We should all try to make eating right as important as any other part of family life," says Michel Nischan.

Michel and his wife, Lori, are committed to feeding their five kids as healthfully as they can, and to putting their muscle where their mouths are: Five years ago they planted an impressive organic garden in their Connecticut backyard. They eat from it all year long, and what the family can't consume, pickle, or otherwise preserve, they share with neighbors.

As a natural outgrowth of his abiding interest in eating seasonally and locally, Michel is the chef/owner of the Dressing Room, a restaurant in Westport, Connecticut, devoted to serving local, sustainably grown food. The restaurant's mission statement: "We believe that the food we grow and cook—in the place that we call home—defines who we are." He is also the author of the award-winning cookbooks *Taste: Pure and Simple* and *Homegrown: Pure and Simple*.

Certainly the food he cooks now and the food he ate as a boy define Michel. When he was growing up, he says, his mother planted a garden that covered the entire backyard all the way to the sliding glass doors of the house. She had grown up on a farm in Missouri and brought her culinary roots with her when the family settled in an Illinois town. The lessons learned in that garden stayed with Michel even as he made his way in the world cooking at high-end restaurants in the Midwest and then the East.

"Ours was the house where other kids came to eat supper," he recalls. "Because of my mother's natural generosity, she welcomed our friends, and I think that's important." Today, the Nischans welcome others to their table, too, and Michel believes that this is a way to get people cooking again.

"I encourage you to keep it easy," he says with a big grin. "Go to the farmer's market and buy two dozen tomatoes, slice them up, and serve them with good olive oil and good salt. Suddenly you're a genius! Or grill some asparagus and serve it with cheese and great bread."

His plan is to wean us off processed food, and, he reasons, when you serve fresh food with a story (where you bought it; where it's from, for instance), it kicks off the conversation. And yet, he is not against buying a take-out entrée and augmenting it with sides featuring fruits and vegetables bought at the farmer's market. "It's a way to make the meal easier by not having to prepare everything from scratch, and that primes the pump for cooking at home more often."

"It's time to get people back into the kitchen," he says.

> "Go to the farmer's market and buy two dozen tomatoes, slice them up, and serve them with good olive oil and good salt. Suddenly you're a genius!"

Michel Nischan's Recipes

- **Tangy Autumn Greens** (page 34)
- **Pumpkin Soup with Crispy Sage Leaves** (page 62)
- **Lemon Pepper Dry Rub Ribs with Garden Vegetable Barbecue Sauce** (page 93)
- **Two Skillet Roasted Herbed Chicken with Oven Fries** (page 122)
- **Yogurt & Citrus Turkey Breast with Grilled Tomato & Wax Bean Salad** (page 134)
- **Spicy Grilled Snapper with Lemongrass & Ginger** (page 146)
- **Garlic-Orange Spinach** (page 173)
- **Pumpkin & Blueberry Tart** (page 255)

Rack of Lamb with Roasted Potatoes & Honey-Cider Carrots

Chef: Rori Trovato

The lamb, cooked on a bed of potatoes and carrots, is ready in about half an hour.

1 rack of lamb, trimmed (French-style)
Salt and freshly ground pepper
2 Tbsp. Dijon mustard
1 Tbsp. chopped fresh rosemary
6 or 7 baby potatoes
2 Tbsp. extra-virgin olive oil
6 to 8 baby carrots or 4 large carrots
　(peeled, scrubbed, and quartered)
2 Tbsp. honey
1 Tbsp. apple cider

1 Preheat oven to 400°. Rub lamb generously with salt and pepper and brush with mustard. Pat with rosemary.

2 Place potatoes in a small baking pan and toss with olive oil; add salt and pepper to taste. Bake 10 minutes. Set lamb upright in same pan and add carrots. Roast 25 to 30 minutes for medium-rare (internal temperature should read 145°). Remove lamb from pan and let rest 10 minutes before carving. Slice between each rib to make 8 or 9 small chops.

3 Remove potatoes. Combine honey and apple cider and toss with carrots in pan. Serve vegetables with lamb.

Serves 2.

Grilled Lamb Chops
with Orange–Rosemary Rub
& Grilled Vegetables

Chef: Rori Trovato

Looking for a sensational dinner for one? This elegant and simple dish is a great solution.

1 small russet or baking potato
1 zucchini, sliced lengthwise
1 yellow squash, sliced lengthwise
1 Tbsp. olive oil
Kosher salt and freshly ground black
   pepper
Zest of 1 orange
1 Tbsp. finely chopped rosemary
1 small garlic clove, finely chopped
3 loin lamb chops

1 Place potato in a medium stockpot over high heat, and add enough water to cover. Bring to a boil and cook until potato is fork-tender, about 25 minutes; remove from water and let cool. When cool enough to handle, cut lengthwise into 4 slices. Brush potato wedges, zucchini, and yellow squash with olive oil; season with salt and pepper to taste, and set aside.

2 Meanwhile, preheat grill to high heat. In a small bowl, combine orange zest, rosemary, garlic, and salt; set aside. Season lamb chops with salt and pepper, and grill one side 3 to 5 minutes for medium-rare to medium. Place prepared vegetables on grill and cook until tender, about 7 minutes, turning as needed. Turn chops over and place half the orange mixture on top. Cook another 3 to 5 minutes, flip over, and transfer to a warm plate. Top with remaining orange mixture and serve with vegetables.

Serves 1.

Lamb Tagine with Preserved Lemons & Green Olives

Created by Moira Hodgson

Serve this glamorous dish on a bed of couscous
with a shower of chopped cilantro.

2 ½ pounds boneless lamb shoulder, cut into 1 ½-inch pieces

Sea salt, table salt, and freshly ground pepper

2 Tbsp. olive oil

1 tsp. ground cumin

1 tsp. ground coriander

1 tsp. turmeric

½ tsp. sweet paprika

1 medium onion, finely chopped

2 garlic cloves, minced

½ pound cracked or whole green olives, pitted

¼ cup chopped Middle Eastern–style salt-preserved lemon (about 1 lemon)

Fresh lemon juice to taste (optional)

½ cup chopped fresh cilantro leaves

3 cups cooked couscous, to serve

1 One day ahead, trim excess fat from lamb. Season meat with ½ tsp. salt and ¼ tsp. pepper. Heat olive oil in a large, heavy-bottomed casserole, then add lamb and sprinkle with cumin, coriander, turmeric, and paprika. Sauté 5 minutes over moderate heat (meat doesn't need to be browned). Add onion and garlic; sauté 1 minute. Add 3 cups water, stir, and bring to a boil. Cover and simmer 1 hour or until tender. Let cool and refrigerate overnight.

2 On the day of serving, preheat oven to 450°. Skim fat from top of stew. Using a slotted spoon, remove lamb chunks and place in a large ovenproof serving dish. Transfer lamb stew liquid to a saucepan and reserve. Bake meat 15 to 20 minutes, or until browned.

3 Meanwhile, blanch olives 1 minute in enough boiling water to cover them (this removes excess salt). Drain and add olives to stew liquid in saucepan; bring to a boil. Cook until reduced and slightly thickened, about 10 minutes, then stir in preserved lemon.

Season to taste with table salt and pepper. Add fresh lemon juice, if using. Pour sauce over lamb, sprinkle with cilantro, and serve with couscous.

Makes 4 servings.

The tagine embodies the regional cooking of Morocco, Tunisia, and Algeria, where it's made in an earthenware pot with a conical lid.

**Lemon Chicken Scaloppine
in Pine Nut–Parmesan Crust**
(recipe on page 114)

Chapter 5

POULTRY

Lemon Chicken Scaloppine in Pine Nut–Parmesan Crust

Chef: Rori Trovato

These are like chicken fingers for adults.

4 boneless, skinless chicken breast halves
1 cup all-purpose flour
2 ½ tsp. salt
1 tsp. freshly ground pepper
3 eggs, lightly beaten
1 ½ cups dry bread crumbs or panko
2 lemons
½ cup grated Parmesan cheese
½ cup coarsely chopped pine nuts
2 Tbsp. chopped basil
2 Tbsp. butter
2 Tbsp. extra-virgin olive oil

1 Using a meat mallet or rolling pin, pound chicken breasts between 2 pieces of waxed paper or plastic wrap until they are ¼ inch thick.

2 Combine flour, 1 tsp. salt, and pepper on a large plate. Put eggs on a separate plate. On a third plate, combine bread crumbs, zest from 1 lemon (2 tsp.), 1 tsp. salt, cheese, pine nuts, and basil. Sprinkle chicken with remaining ½ tsp. salt. Coat both sides in flour, then eggs (allowing excess to drip off), then bread crumb mixture, pressing mixture in slightly.

3 In a large skillet over a medium flame, heat 1 Tbsp. butter and 1 Tbsp. olive oil. When pan is hot, add 1 to 2 chicken breasts; cook 2 to 3 minutes on each side, until golden and cooked through. Remove and keep warm on a plate tented with foil. Add more butter and oil to skillet with each batch. Cut remaining unpeeled lemon into large wedges. Squeeze 2 wedges over chicken before serving and place remaining wedges on platter with chicken.

Makes 4 servings.

Sautéed Chicken with Cherry Tomatoes

Chef: Nina Simonds

For a light dish that takes advantage of summer's fresh ingredients, try this.

3 Tbsp. extra-virgin olive oil

6 boneless, skinless chicken breast* halves (about 1½ pounds)

4 garlic cloves, smashed and coarsely chopped

6 shallots, peeled and coarsely chopped

2 pints cherry or grape tomatoes, rinsed and drained

1 tsp. dried oregano

¾ cup dry white wine

Salt and freshly ground black pepper

1 pound spinach angel-hair pasta, cooked according to package directions

*You can substitute boneless chicken thighs for the boneless breasts. Cook as directed in step 1, then add the seared thighs in step 2, and cook until opaque and tender, 15 to 20 minutes.

1 In a 12-inch skillet, a Dutch oven, or a lidded casserole, heat oil over medium-high heat. Add half the chicken and cook until golden brown, about 6 minutes total, turning midway through cooking time. Remove with tongs and brown remaining chicken breasts. Set aside.

2 Reduce heat to medium. Add garlic and shallots, and sauté until fragrant, about 15 seconds. Add cherry tomatoes, oregano, white wine, ½ tsp. salt, and ¼ tsp. pepper, and sauté until wine reduces by a third, about 4 minutes, shaking the pan from time to time. Return chicken to pan, cover, and simmer until chicken is cooked through and no longer pink, 5 to 7 minutes. Adjust seasoning to taste. Serve chicken over angel-hair pasta.

Makes 6 servings.

Great for a busy family, this easy meal is guaranteed to please even the pickiest eaters.

115

Lemon–Olive Chicken with Vegetable Tagine

Chef: Marcus Samuelsson

This is a dish of bright, bold flavors. The jalapeños add a fiery topnote.

CHICKEN

One (4- to 5-pound) chicken
1 tsp. salt
10 green olives
5 black olives
4 garlic cloves, smashed
1 Tbsp. grated lemon zest
2 shallots, roughly chopped
One (3-inch) piece ginger, peeled
2 Tbsp. olive oil
Juice of 2 lemons (about ¼ cup)
1 Tbsp. ras el hanout*

*You can find ras el hanout, a Moroccan spice blend, at www.zamourispices.com.

TAGINE

2 parsnips, peeled and cut into 1-inch chunks
2 baking potatoes, peeled and cut into 1-inch cubes
2 beets, peeled and cut into 1-inch cubes
½ cup olive oil
2 eggplants (skin on), cut into 2-inch cubes
1 medium Spanish onion, cut into 1-inch cubes
4 garlic cloves, minced
½ cup green olives, halved and pitted
2 jalapeño chilies, seeds and ribs removed, finely chopped
1 tsp. ground turmeric
1 tsp. ground cumin
2 cups vegetable stock or broth
Salt
2 Tbsp. chopped parsley
½ cup raisins

1 To make the chicken: Preheat oven to 400°. Rub body and neck cavities of chicken with salt; sprinkle skin with salt. Stuff cavities with olives, garlic, lemon zest, shallots, and ginger. In a small bowl, combine olive oil, lemon juice, and ras el hanout; rub all over chicken breasts and legs.

2 Truss chicken. Place on a rack in a roasting pan; roast until an instant-read thermometer inserted in thickest part of thigh registers 160°, 60 to 70 minutes.

3 Transfer to a platter. Let rest 10 to 15 minutes before carving. Serve with vegetable tagine.

4 To make the tagine: Combine parsnips, potatoes, and beets in a Dutch oven or other large pot, cover with water, and bring to a boil. Reduce heat and simmer until tender, 15 to 20 minutes. Drain and set aside.

5 Heat olive oil in a large, deep sauté pan over medium-high heat. Add eggplant, onion, garlic, olives, and jalapeños; reduce heat to medium and sauté until eggplant is tender, about 10 minutes.

6 Stir in turmeric, cumin, stock, potatoes, parsnips, beets, and ½ tsp. salt; bring to a boil. Reduce heat to low and simmer, stirring occasionally, until vegetables are tender, 15 to 20 minutes.

7 Remove from heat. Stir in parsley and raisins; season to taste before serving.

Makes 4 servings.

Cinnamon Curry Roasted Chicken with Tomato Yogurt Sauce

Chef: Rori Trovato

It's a little bit sweet, a little bit daring. It's cinnamon, and it's probably sitting right there in your pantry.

CHICKEN

One (4-pound) roasting chicken
1 tsp. cumin seeds
½ tsp. black peppercorns
½ tsp. coriander seeds
3 green cardamom pods
1 Tbsp. curry powder
1 tsp. ground cinnamon
½ tsp. red pepper flakes
1 head garlic, cloves separated and
    unpeeled, plus 6 cloves, peeled
2 Tbsp. finely grated ginger
1 Tbsp. olive oil
1½ tsp. salt
2 shallots, unpeeled and quartered
3 cinnamon sticks
1 cup chicken broth

SAUCE

1 cup plain low-fat yogurt, room
    temperature
2 tomatoes, seeded and chopped
3 Tbsp. chopped cilantro

1 To make chicken: Preheat oven to 450°. Pat chicken dry with paper towels. Place on a rack in a small roasting pan or baking dish. Set aside.

2 In a small frying pan over medium heat, combine cumin seeds, black peppercorns, coriander seeds, and cardamom pods. Swirl until lightly toasted and fragrant, 2 to 4 minutes. Remove from heat and cool slightly; grind using a mortar and pestle. (To save time, or if you don't have equipment, use preground spices and toast in pan 45 seconds.) Mix with curry powder, cinnamon, and red pepper flakes.

3 Finely chop peeled garlic cloves and combine with ginger and olive oil in a small bowl. Rub mixture over entire chicken. Sprinkle with salt, then with spice mixture. Place unpeeled garlic, shallots, and cinnamon sticks inside chicken cavity. Tie legs with kitchen string. Roast 30 minutes before basting with ½ cup chicken broth. Roast 20 minutes more, then baste with remaining ½ cup broth. Continue cooking until juices run clear when chicken is pierced with a knife and meat is no longer pink, about 1 hour and 15 minutes total. Remove from oven and cool slightly.

4 To make sauce: Transfer juices from pan into a saucepan and bring to a boil. Reduce heat. Slowly add in yogurt, stirring constantly with a whisk so yogurt doesn't curdle. Remove from heat. Add most of the tomatoes and cilantro, setting some aside to garnish top of chicken. Serve with sauce on side.

Makes 2 to 3 servings.

Moroccan Chicken over Couscous

Chef: Rori Trovato

Talk about easy! With only a few ingredients, and couscous that cooks in minutes, dinner is ready and totally satisfying.

CHICKEN

8 chicken thighs

2 tsp. ground cumin

Salt and freshly ground pepper

2 Tbsp. extra-virgin olive oil

2 cups chicken stock

¼ cup chopped mint, plus whole leaves

3 Tbsp. sliced or chopped kalamata olives

COUSCOUS

2 cups chicken stock

1 ⅓ cups couscous

½ tsp. salt

1 To make the chicken: Rub the chicken thighs with cumin and a generous sprinkling of salt and pepper. In a large, high-sided skillet or Dutch oven, heat the olive oil over medium-high heat. Add the chicken thighs and brown the skin, 7 to 10 minutes per side. Add the 2 cups of chicken stock. Bring to a boil, then cover and reduce the heat to medium-low; allow the stock to simmer 20 minutes. Add the chopped mint and the sliced or chopped olives. Continue cooking 15 to 20 minutes, or until the chicken is tender. Remove the lid, increase the heat to high, and reduce the sauce 3 to 5 minutes, until slightly thickened. Add additional salt, if desired.

2 To make the couscous: In a medium saucepan, heat the 2 cups of chicken stock until just boiling, add the couscous and salt and cover. Remove from the heat and let stand 5 minutes. Fluff with a fork.

3 Serve the couscous on a platter with the chicken on top. Spoon the sauce over it and garnish with the whole mint leaves.

Makes 4 servings.

African Chicken in Peanut Sauce

Chef: Norma Jean Darden

The chicken finishes cooking in a rich and creamy peanut sauce for a simple dish that transforms supper into something memorable.

SPICE RUB

¾ tsp. salt

¾ tsp. ground black pepper

1 ½ tsp. chopped garlic

1 ½ tsp. onion powder

¾ tsp. ground cayenne pepper

CHICKEN

4 pounds bone-in chicken pieces, skin removed

3 Tbsp. vegetable oil

PEANUT SAUCE

1 small onion, finely diced

½ red bell pepper, seeded and finely diced

½ green bell pepper, seeded and finely diced

1 medium carrot, finely diced

1 garlic clove, minced

1 tsp. finely diced and seeded jalapeño chili

4 cups (32 ounces) chicken broth

½ cup smooth peanut butter

1 Tbsp. tomato paste

½ tomato, seeded and diced

1 tsp. chopped fresh thyme leaves (or ½ tsp. dried)

½ tsp. peeled, grated fresh ginger

½ cup well-mixed coconut milk

½ tsp. salt

¼ tsp. finely ground black pepper

¼ cup chopped parsley, for garnish

1. Stir together the spice rub ingredients and rub onto chicken pieces.

2. Heat 1 Tbsp. oil in a large nonstick skillet over medium-high heat. Working in batches, add half the chicken and brown on all sides, taking care not to burn the spices. Transfer browned pieces to a platter and set aside. Brown remaining chicken and transfer to platter.

3. With a paper towel, wipe skillet dry; then add remaining 2 Tbsp. oil. Add onion, red and green bell peppers, carrot, garlic, and jalapeño chili. Cook until vegetables are soft, about 5 minutes. Add chicken broth and simmer until reduced by half, about 20 minutes. Reduce heat to medium-low, stir in remaining sauce ingredients, and simmer 2 minutes. Return browned chicken to skillet. Cook 25 to 30 minutes, or until chicken is tender and cooked through, stirring frequently to prevent sauce from sticking. Turn chicken pieces over midway through cooking time. Garnish with parsley.

Makes 6 servings.

121

Two Skillet Roasted Herbed Chicken with Oven Fries

Chef: Michel Nischan

Cooking chicken between two skillets speeds up the process, says Chef Michel Nischan, and best of all, you get a moist, tender dish.

CHICKEN

One (3- to 3¼-pound) chicken
1 bunch thyme
1 bunch sage
½ tsp. salt
¼ tsp. freshly ground pepper

FRIES

6 medium Yukon Gold potatoes, thinly
  sliced
3 tsp. grapeseed or canola oil
½ tsp. salt
¼ tsp. freshly ground pepper
1 small onion, finely diced
Eight (3-inch) rosemary sprigs
6 sage sprigs, with 3 to 4 leaves each
Canola oil nonstick cooking spray

1 To make chicken: Preheat oven to 425° with a 10-inch cast-iron skillet inside. Remove giblets and neck. Rinse chicken with cold water; drain, then pat dry with paper towels. Butterfly by cutting along both sides of the backbone with kitchen scissors; discard backbone. Lay chicken out flat, skin side down. With the heel of your hand, firmly press breastbone to flatten chicken; turn skin side up.

2 Divide thyme and sage each into 4 equal portions. Loosen skin from chicken over breasts and thighs; insert thyme under skin over each breast and thigh.

3 Over medium-high heat, heat a 12-inch cast-iron skillet. Season chicken with salt and pepper. Place chicken skin side down in skillet, with leg portion closest to the handle. Cook until skin is lightly browned, about 4 minutes. Turn chicken over; place sage on each breast and thigh. Remove 10-inch skillet from oven; place on top of chicken (bottom down) so handles match.

4 Pan-roast chicken 30 minutes. Remove top skillet. Cook chicken 10 more minutes. It is done when meat thermometer inserted in thickest part of thigh (without touching the bone) reads 175° to 180° and juices run clear when pierced with a sharp knife. Let chicken stand 10 minutes before carving.

5 To make fries: Preheat oven to 400° with a 12-inch cast-iron skillet inside. In a large bowl, toss potatoes, 2 tsp. oil, ¼ tsp. salt, and pepper.

6 Brush hot skillet with remaining 1 tsp. oil. Place potatoes in skillet. Oven-roast them until browned on bottom, about 20 minutes. Turn them over and sprinkle with onion. Lightly coat rosemary and sage sprigs with cooking spray; add to potatoes. Oven-roast potatoes until browned and tender, 15 to 20 minutes. Sprinkle with remaining ¼ tsp. salt. Stack potatoes with herbs on a warm platter.

Makes 4 servings.

Pecan-Coated Fried Chicken

Chef: Lee Bailey

We think the crunchy pecan coating makes fried chicken better than ever.

6 boneless, skinless chicken breast
halves
1 ½ cups buttermilk
2 cups pecans
1 ⅓ cups flour
1 ½ tsp. salt
½ tsp. freshly ground pepper
Olive oil, for frying

1 Cut each breast half diagonally into 6 pieces. Place the chicken in a bowl, cover with the butter-milk, and marinate for 20 minutes at room temperature.

2 In a food processor, pulse the pecans, flour, salt, and pepper until the nuts are roughly chopped. Transfer the pecan mixture to a bowl and, one at a time, coat the chicken pieces thoroughly. Set the coated pieces on a baking sheet, cover with plastic wrap, and refrigerate for at least 30 minutes.

3 Fill a cast-iron skillet halfway with olive oil and heat over medium-high heat until hot but not smoking. Cook the chicken about 2 minutes per side, or until dark golden. Drain the chicken on paper towels and serve hot.

Makes 6 servings.

Grilled Sesame-Marinated Duck Breasts with Hoisin Sauce

Created by Moira Hodgson

Who needs a stove? It's summertime and the grilling is easy.

DUCK

2 garlic cloves, chopped

¼ cup sesame oil

2 Tbsp. soy sauce

4 boneless duck breast halves (about 7 ounces each)

¼ cup fresh rosemary, plus some sprigs for garnish

2 Tbsp. hoisin sauce, plus more for dipping

SALAD

2 Tbsp. fresh lemon juice (about 1 lemon)

1 Tbsp. balsamic vinegar, or to taste

¼ cup extra-virgin olive oil

Salt and freshly ground black pepper

4 cups bitter greens (arugula, mizuna, frisée, or a combination)

2 ripe mangoes, peeled and chopped

1 To make duck: In a small bowl, combine garlic, sesame oil, and soy sauce; set aside. Remove any loose fat from duck breasts, and score skin lightly with a sharp knife (take care not to cut into the flesh). Place breasts in a nonreactive dish just large enough to hold them. Coat with garlic mixture and sprinkle with rosemary. Cover and refrigerate overnight or at least 4 hours, turning occasionally.

2 Bring duck breasts to room temperature; preheat gas grill to medium-high, or prepare a charcoal grill for direct grilling over medium-high heat.

3 Place duck breasts on grill skin side down. Cook 5 to 8 minutes per side for rare and 8 to 10 minutes for medium-rare, turning and brushing with hoisin sauce about halfway through cooking time. Skin should be crisp and brown but not burned.

4 To make salad: In a small bowl, combine lemon juice, balsamic vinegar, olive oil, ¾ tsp. salt, and ¼ tsp. pepper. Adjust seasoning to taste.

5 Place breasts on a platter and let rest 3 to 4 minutes. Meanwhile, place greens and mangoes in a salad bowl and toss with dressing. Cut duck into slices about ¼ inch thick, and garnish with rosemary sprigs. Serve with salad and a small bowl of hoisin sauce on the side for dipping.

Makes 4 servings.

Maple-Glazed Whole Duck with Savoy Cabbage

Chef: Govind Armstrong

If you've never cooked a whole duck, don't wait another day. The maple glaze is lovely with the rich meat, and the cabbage is a delicious extra.

DUCK

1 whole (3½-pound) duck (available at Whole Foods, nationwide)

1 small yellow onion, sliced in half

1 head garlic, cloves separated and unpeeled

1 bunch fresh thyme

1 bunch fresh parsley

1 bunch fresh rosemary

2 Tbsp. kosher salt

1 Tbsp. pepper

½ cup red wine vinegar

1 cup Vermont maple syrup

CABBAGE

2 Tbsp. canola oil

1 Tbsp. butter

2 celery stalks, finely diced

2 large carrots, peeled and finely diced

1 medium yellow onion, diced

4 garlic cloves, thinly sliced

2 heads Savoy cabbage (cored and white ribs removed), blanched

Kosher salt and pepper to taste

1 To make duck: Preheat oven to 350°. Remove innards from cavity of duck and wash bird thoroughly. Fill duck with onion, garlic, herbs, salt, and pepper. In a small bowl, combine vinegar and maple syrup; brush outside of bird liberally with mixture.

2 Place duck on roasting rack and cook 1 hour, glazing periodically.

3 To make cabbage: In a large sauté pan over medium heat, heat oil. Add butter, celery, and carrots; sauté 5 minutes. Add onion and garlic; sauté another 5 minutes, or until onion is translucent. Add cabbage, then season with salt and pepper. Place on a platter and serve roasted duck on top.

Makes 10 servings.

Cornish Game Hens with Wild Rice & Mushroom Stuffing

Created by Sheila Bridges

These tiny birds, stuffed with a mellow, earthy blend of mushrooms and wild rice, are an elegant main course.

CORNISH GAME HENS
8 cornish game hens (1 pound each)
Kosher salt
Cracked black pepper

STUFFING
1 ½ ounces dried porcini mushrooms
6 Tbsp. (¾ stick) unsalted butter
¼ cup finely chopped onion
⅓ cup finely chopped celery
1 cup finely chopped fresh mushrooms
 (shiitake, morel, chanterelle, etc.)*
3 cups cooked wild rice
¼ cup chopped fresh parsley
¼ cup chopped fresh sage
1 tsp. kosher salt
½ tsp. cracked black pepper

*6 shiitake mushrooms make 1 cup chopped.

1 Preheat oven to 350°. Remove and discard game hen necks and giblets; rinse and pat dry. Sprinkle generously with salt and pepper. Set aside.

2 To make stuffing: In a small bowl, soak porcini mushrooms in 1 cup of water for 25 minutes. Strain mushrooms and liquid through a coffee filter placed in a strainer over a bowl. Reserve liquid (about ⅔ cup). Rinse and chop mushrooms; set aside. In a large sauté pan over medium heat, melt 3 Tbsp. butter. When butter is foamy, add onion, celery, and fresh and reserved mushrooms. Stir until onion is soft and translucent, about 8 minutes. Add rice, herbs, salt, and pepper. Moisten slightly with about 3 Tbsp. reserved mushroom water, depending on dryness. Makes 4½ cups stuffing.

3 Melt remaining butter and set aside. Gently fill bird cavities with stuffing. Fold excess skin over opening and tie legs together. Place hens, with ample space between them, on two 12" x 19" baking sheets. Brush hens generously with butter. Bake about 1 hour.

Makes 8 servings.

At the Table with Art Smith
A HEART AS BIG AS THE WHOLE OUTDOORS

Never a man to do things in a small way, when Art Smith constructed a substantial outdoor kitchen in the backyard of his Chicago condominium complex, it quickly became a gathering place for his neighbors, friends, and family. And for neighbors of neighbors and friends of friends!

"We cook there all summer," he says, "and even into the fall and winter. In fact, in the fall, the kitchen becomes chili-and-grilled-pizza central." Art's outdoor kitchen includes a wood-and-gas-fired oven, a large grill, and a tandoor oven, which may be a common sight in Northern India and Pakistan but is a novelty in Chicago.

The inclusion of the tandoor is not surprising. Art knows his way around outdoor and indoor kitchens everywhere. Oprah's personal chef and the former executive chef for Senator Bob Graham when he was governor of Florida, Art is also a respected cookbook author and celebrity chef who has worked all over the world. During his travels he found that cooking outdoors is universal—and universally loved.

"It's not an American thing," Art says. "The Italians have incredible outdoor ovens, as do the Croats, who cook one-dish meals to die for in large outdoor ovens." In South Africa, he says, the backyard grill is called a *braai*, which is a term that refers to the act of cooking over a hot fire, the grill itself, and the party—not unlike our own American term "barbecue."

Art took great care when building his outdoor kitchen and has a word of advice for anyone considering one: Include a refrigerator and ample work space if at all possible. This way, you can prepare the entire meal outdoors. If you have to mess up your indoor kitchen to cook outdoors, he reasons, you will be less inclined to do so and the novelty will soon wear thin.

> Everyone is attracted to the grill "like moths to light."

"Nowadays we have so many choices when it comes to what we cook outdoors," he says. "Even hot dogs are varied! But it's not just hamburgers and hot dogs anymore." Art remembers the fun he and his neighbors had when he taught them how to "throw naan," a type of Indian hearth bread, using the tandoor oven. And as exciting as food cooked outdoors might be, the meal itself tends to be unhurried and casual.

"People expect nothing more than something hot off the grill," he says. "And then all you need is a salad and maybe some cookies and fruit." What's more, he continues, everyone is attracted to the grill "like moths to light," so just the act of firing it up tends to be communal.

"We're also drawn to the craft of it," says Art. "By this I mean you have to think about the wood or the charcoal, the heat intensity, the grill marks on the food." He admits these challenges seem to attract middle-aged men more than some other demographics.

This country boy who grew up in rural Florida muses that when you live with as much concrete as he and so many other Americans do in cities and populated suburbs, "You yearn for green, but that doesn't mean you want a farm." The idea of spending time out of doors, cooking, eating, and visiting, is overwhelmingly appealing.

"We dug up the concrete in the condo's backyard for the kitchen, and let me tell you: It's the focal point of our little community."

The good thing about the outdoors is that it's big enough for everyone.

Art Smith's Recipes
- **Sweet Potato Salad** (page 32)
- **Cabbage-Wrapped Salmon Steamed in Wine** (page 150)
- **Focaccia with Caramelized Onions, Goat Cheese, & Rosemary** (page 218)
- **Art Smith's 12-Layer Chocolate Cake** (page 234)

Organic Turkey Stuffed with Brown & Wild Rice, Dried Cranberries, & Walnuts

Chef: Rori Trovato

We love USDA-certified organic turkeys for their good flavor and succulence. Plus, they cook more quickly than their conventionally raised counterparts.

2 Tbsp. extra-virgin olive oil

1 large yellow onion, chopped into ¼-inch dice

4 celery stalks, chopped into ¼-inch dice

1 ½ cups (6 ounces) sliced white button or cremini mushrooms

3 Tbsp. chopped fresh sage (or 1½ tsp. dried)

¾ cup dried cranberries

¾ cup chopped walnuts

2 cups prepackaged mixed brown and wild rice

4 cups chicken broth

Salt and freshly ground black pepper

One (12-pound) organic turkey

1 In a 4-quart pot, heat 1 Tbsp. olive oil over medium-high heat. Add onion and celery and cook, stirring occasionally, until tender, about 5 minutes. Add mushrooms and continue cooking 3 more minutes. Add sage, cranberries, walnuts, rice, broth, 1 tsp. salt, and ¼ tsp. pepper. Raise heat to high and bring to a boil, then reduce heat to medium-low, cover, and cook 45 minutes, without lifting lid. Remove from heat.

2 Meanwhile, preheat oven to 325°. Remove neck and bag of giblets from turkey cavity, then rinse turkey inside and out and pat dry with paper towels. Fill neck cavity with some cooked rice mixture—don't stuff too tight. Fold neck skin over rice and fasten to turkey back with 1 or 2 skewers. Spoon remaining stuffing into body cavity—again, don't stuff too tight. (If any rice mixture remains, place in an ovenproof dish and cover with foil.) Fold skin over opening. Tie legs and tail end of bird together with kitchen string. Rub remaining 1 Tbsp. olive oil over skin of turkey and season generously with salt and pepper.

3 Place turkey on a rack in a roasting pan. Roast about 3½ hours, basting with juices and drippings in bottom of pan during last hour of roasting. Remove from oven and let sit 15 minutes before serving.

4 Transfer turkey to a large platter. With a spoon, transfer rice from turkey to a bowl. To reheat extra rice, place ovenproof dish in oven with turkey during last 30 minutes of cooking until heated through. Serve at once.

Makes 8 to 10 servings.

The stuffing can be made a day in advance and placed in the turkey just before serving.

133

Yogurt & Citrus Turkey Breast with Grilled Tomato & Wax Bean Salad

Chef: Michel Nischan

The orange zest–and–yogurt marinade keeps this dish moist and tender.

TURKEY
2 pounds (½-inch-thick) turkey cutlets
Salt and freshly ground pepper
Zest and juice of 2 large oranges
2 cups plain low-fat organic yogurt
2 Tbsp. grated fresh ginger
¼ cup packed fresh mint leaves, chopped

BEAN SALAD
½ pound green beans, trimmed
½ pound wax beans, trimmed
Sea salt and freshly ground pepper
3 large ripe tomatoes, cut into ½-inch-thick slices
¼ cup aged balsamic vinegar
¼ cup extra-virgin olive oil

1 To make turkey: Place cutlets between doubled sheets of plastic wrap. Using a meat mallet or rolling pin, pound cutlets to ¼-inch thickness. Season with salt and pepper.

2 In a small bowl, combine orange zest and juice, yogurt, ginger, and mint; stir until blended. Pour yogurt mixture into a large resealable plastic bag; add turkey cutlets and turn to coat thoroughly. Refrigerate 2 hours.

3 Heat a large panini griddle or Foreman grill to high (with drip tray in place). Remove cutlets from marinade; allow excess yogurt to drip off. In batches, place cutlets on grill, cover, and cook until cooked through, about 2 minutes. Keep warm in oven.

4 To make bean salad: Heat a panini griddle or Foreman grill. In batches, arrange beans in a single layer on griddle. Cover and cook until just tender, 4 to 5 minutes. Sprinkle with salt and pepper to taste and set aside.

5 Sprinkle tomato slices with salt and pepper to taste; grill until just heated through, about 1 minute.

6 In a small bowl, whisk vinegar and oil until blended. On each of 6 plates layer tomato slices and beans, drizzling each layer with vinaigrette. Top with turkey cutlets.

Makes 6 servings.

"You hear the ingredient list, and you know it's going to taste great," says Michel Nischan.

134

Spicy Shrimp with Basil
(recipe on page 156)

Chapter 6

FISH & SEAFOOD

Poached Cod with Olive & Orange Vinaigrette

Chef: Rori Trovato

A lively vinaigrette made with fresh-squeezed orange juice and salty black olives perks up the flavor of mild codfish.

VINAIGRETTE

1 Tbsp. minced shallots
½ cup pitted kalamata olives, sliced in half
¼ cup orange juice (about 1 orange)
3 Tbsp. olive oil
Kosher salt and pepper to taste

FISH

2 cups dry white wine
1 Tbsp. fennel seeds
¼ cup orange juice (about 1 orange)
3 Tbsp. lemon juice (about 1 lemon)
2 bay leaves
Four (6-ounce) cod fillets
Pinch of kosher salt

1 To make vinaigrette: In a medium bowl, combine shallots, olives, and orange juice; mix well. Slowly stir in olive oil. Season with salt and pepper, if desired. Set aside.

2 To make fish: In a large, deep skillet, combine 1 cup water, wine, fennel seeds, orange juice, lemon juice, and bay leaves. Bring to a boil, reduce heat, and simmer 15 minutes. Add fish and sprinkle with salt. Poach just until opaque, about 7 minutes. Remove fish with a slotted spatula and transfer to a serving platter. Drizzle with vinaigrette.

Makes 4 servings.

Atlantic cod is over-fished; use Pacific cod if available. For a nonalcoholic recipe, substitute vegetable broth for the wine.

Grilled Redfish with Red Rice & Lemon Butter Sauce

Chef: Ralph Brennan

The redfish with rice is a meal in itself—and a very good one. The lemony sauce is an unexpected bonus that brings the dish together.

SAUCE

1 cup dry white wine
3/4 cup fresh lemon juice
1 tsp. cider vinegar
1 tsp. minced shallot
1 garlic clove, minced
1 tsp. chopped fresh thyme leaves
24 Tbsp. (3 sticks) cold, unsalted butter, cut into tablespoons
1/2 tsp. grated lemon zest
1 tsp. kosher salt
Pinch of freshly ground pepper

RICE

4 Tbsp. unsalted butter
1/2 medium onion, chopped
1 celery stalk, diced
3 small garlic cloves, minced
1 cup long-grain rice
4 green onions, thinly sliced
2 medium tomatoes, diced
1 Tbsp. chopped flat-leaf parsley
One (14-ounce) can chicken broth
1 tsp. kosher salt
3 small bay leaves

FISH

2 Tbsp. olive oil, plus more for greasing
Six (7-ounce) red snapper (or flounder or sea bass) fillets, skin removed
1 tsp. Creole seasoning
2 lemons, cut into 6 wedges each
Flat-leaf parsley sprigs, for garnish

1 To make sauce: In a small saucepan combine wine, lemon juice, vinegar, shallot, garlic, and thyme. Bring to a boil; reduce heat to medium-high and continue to boil until reduced to 1/4 cup, 20 to 25 minutes. Reduce heat to medium-low and add butter, 4 Tbsp. at a time, whisking until just melted. Butter should emulsify and thicken sauce slightly. (If the first batch melts too quickly and thins out sauce, turn heat to low, then continue.) Whisk in lemon zest, salt, and pepper, and set sauce aside.

2 To make rice: In a 3-quart saucepan, melt butter over medium heat. Add onion, celery, and garlic. Cook until softened, about 3 minutes. Stir in rice, green onions, tomatoes, and parsley. Cook 2 minutes, stirring frequently. Stir in 1/4 cup water, chicken broth, salt, and bay leaves, then bring to a boil. Reduce heat; cover and simmer until liquid is absorbed and rice is tender, about 20 minutes. Remove saucepan from heat and let stand.

3 To make fish: Preheat grill or grill pan; grease with olive oil. Brush snapper fillets with olive oil and sprinkle with Creole seasoning. Grill fillets over medium-high heat until opaque throughout, 2 to 3 minutes per side. Grill lemon wedges on medium-high heat until marked on both sides, about 30 seconds per side.

4 Reheat sauce over low heat. Do not allow to simmer, or sauce will separate. Remove bay leaves from rice, then spoon rice onto plates. Top with snapper fillets and sauce. Garnish with grilled lemon wedges and parsley sprigs.

Makes 6 servings.

140

Seared Tuna with Fresh Corn & Wasabi "Cream"

Chef: Rozanne Gold

Food freed from "ingredient overload" can be beautiful, satisfying, and stunningly flavorful. This dish proves it.

3 large ears corn, shucked and kernels removed (about 2 cups)
Salt
1 tsp. wasabi paste
Four (8-ounce) fresh tuna steaks, about ¾ inch thick

1 To a small saucepan with 1¾ cups water, add 1½ cups corn kernels and a large pinch of salt. Bring to a boil; lower heat and cook until very soft, about 20 minutes. Place corn and cooking liquid in a blender; puree until very smooth, adding several Tbsp. water if too thick. Strain through a coarse-mesh sieve into a small bowl. Stir in wasabi paste. Add salt to taste. Makes about 1 cup.

2 Place remaining ½ cup corn kernels in a saucepan with enough water to cover. Cook over medium heat for 10 minutes.

3 Meanwhile, rub salt into both sides of tuna steaks. Coat a large nonstick skillet with cooking spray. Heat skillet over medium-high heat until hot. Add tuna and sear each side, about 3 minutes. Remove tuna from heat and place on a platter.

4 Reheat sauce, adding salt to taste. Drain corn. Pour sauce over fish and scatter cooked corn on top. Serve immediately.

Makes 4 servings.

Sicilian-Style Swordfish

Chef: Mollie Ahlstrand

Skillet-seared swordfish with a sauce of fresh tomatoes, black olives, and capers calls out for a side dish with bold flavors of its own: Try a garlicky sautéed Swiss chard.

Six (6- to 7-ounce) swordfish steaks
½ tsp. salt
¼ tsp. white pepper
Flour
¼ cup extra-virgin olive oil
⅓ cup white wine
2 Tbsp. fresh lemon juice
1 cup diced tomato
¼ cup pitted and chopped black olives
2 Tbsp. chopped fresh Italian parsley
1 Tbsp. coarsely chopped capers
1 Tbsp. chopped fresh oregano

1 Sprinkle both sides of each swordfish steak with salt and pepper. Spread flour on a large plate; dip steaks in flour, covering both sides, and shake off excess.

2 In a 12-inch nonstick skillet, heat olive oil over high heat. Add swordfish and sauté 3 minutes per side, until golden. Add wine, lemon juice, and 2 Tbsp. water; reduce heat to medium. Simmer swordfish 3 minutes, basting steaks occasionally with sauce, until cooked through. Transfer swordfish to a platter; cover and keep warm.

3 Add ½ cup diced tomato, olives, parsley, capers, and oregano to sauce in skillet; bring to a simmer. Top swordfish with sauce and sprinkle with remaining ½ cup tomato.

Makes 6 servings.

143

Swordfish Niçoise

Chef: Lee Bailey

We love pan-fried swordfish served with Mediterranean-style tomatoes and olives.
Add some steamed asparagus and tiny potatoes to complete the meal.

1 ½ tsp. hot red pepper sauce
1 Tbsp. plus ½ tsp. soy sauce
Six (8-ounce) swordfish steaks, about
   ½ inch thick
2 Tbsp. butter, divided
1 pint cherry tomatoes, rinsed and
   stemmed
½ cup niçoise olives

1 Combine the hot pepper sauce and soy sauce. Rub the swordfish steaks with the mixture, using approximately ½ tsp. on each side.

2 Heat a large skillet over high heat. Melt 1 Tbsp. butter and add 3 fish steaks. Sauté approximately 2 minutes on each side, just until the fish is cooked in the center. Remove the fish from the heat and cover with foil to keep warm. Set aside. Repeat with the remaining fish steaks.

3 Add the tomatoes and olives to the pan, and sauté for 1 minute, or until the mixture is warm but the tomatoes are still firm.

4 Garnish the fish with the tomatoes and olives.

Makes 6 servings.

144

Spicy Grilled Snapper with Lemongrass & Ginger

Chef: Michel Nischan

Grill the snapper on top of lemongrass and slather it with an Asian-inspired barbecue sauce. The aroma alone is worth the effort.

BARBECUE SAUCE

1 cup bottled oyster sauce

1 cup mirin (Japanese rice wine)

⅔ cup rice vinegar

2 lemongrass stalks (white part only), peeled and thinly sliced, or grated zest of ½ lemon

¼ cup thinly sliced peeled fresh ginger

2 star anise pods

1 Tbsp. Asian chili sauce or chili paste

SNAPPER

2 red snappers or yellowtail, cleaned and scaled

6 lemongrass stalks, lightly smashed with a mallet, or grated zest of 2 lemons

½ cup thinly sliced peeled fresh ginger

2 limes, thinly sliced

1 yellow onion, thinly sliced

10 lemon verbena sprigs (optional)

1 lemongrass stalk, thinly sliced

1 To make sauce: In a medium saucepan, combine all ingredients. Bring to a simmer over medium heat. Cook 15 to 20 minutes. Strain through a fine-mesh sieve and let cool. Reserve solids.

2 To make snapper: Measure 1 cup barbecue sauce; set aside. With small, sharp knife, make 4 shallow slashes in each side of fish from head to tail. Stuff cavities with reserved solids from sauce. Rub about 1 Tbsp. cooled sauce over each side of fish. Lay 3 lemongrass stalks across bottom of a casserole or baking dish just large enough to hold both fish without stacking. Scatter half of ginger, limes, onion slices, and lemon verbena over bottom of baking dish. (This will provide a flavor base for fish to rest on while marinating.) Lay fish in the baking dish and pour half of remaining sauce on top. Arrange remaining 3 lemongrass stalks, ginger, lime, onion, and lemon verbena on top. Cover tightly and refrigerate fish and reserved sauce 8 hours or overnight.

3 Prepare a fire in a charcoal grill, or preheat a gas grill to medium-hot. Remove layer of lemongrass and lay it on grill, avoiding hottest sections. Lay fish side by side on top of lemongrass (to provide flavor and prevent sticking). Grill fish 6 to 8 minutes. Baste each snapper with about 2 Tbsp. remaining sauce. Arrange lemongrass from bottom of dish next to fish on grill. Using a large spatula, roll fish onto lemongrass, exposing uncooked side to heat of grill. (Rolling method keeps tender fish from falling apart.) Sprinkle with thinly sliced lemongrass. Cook fish 4 to 6 minutes longer, basting with remaining sauce. Using a spatula, roll fish onto a baking sheet. (To broil fish: Preheat broiler and broiler pan. Lightly spray pan with nonstick spray. Remove one fish from marinade; place on pan and generously baste with reserved sauce. Broil 5 inches from heat source 5 minutes; baste with sauce and broil 5 minutes more. Turn fish over, generously baste with sauce, and broil 3 to 5 minutes more, or until fish flakes easily when tested with a small, sharp knife. Repeat with remaining fish.) Serve immediately.

Makes 4 servings.

Maple-Brined Salmon with Corn Relish & Sage Potatoes

Chef: Matt Steigerwald

We're always looking for new ways to serve salmon, and this maple-brined preparation is one of the most satisfying.

SALMON

¾ cup maple syrup

¼ cup plus ¼ teaspoon salt

1 Tbsp. whole black peppercorns

1 bay leaf

Eight (5- to 6-ounce) salmon fillets (preferably wild)

2 Tbsp. canola oil

RELISH

1 tsp. salt

2 cups fresh corn kernels

¾ cup chopped shallots

2 Tbsp. white wine vinegar

1 small red bell pepper, minced

¾ cup chopped parsley

2 Tbsp. extra-virgin olive oil

1 Tbsp. chopped fresh sage

1 tsp. minced garlic

¼ tsp. freshly ground pepper

POTATOES

2 pounds new or fingerling potatoes, halved

12 garlic cloves, lightly smashed with side of knife

8 fresh sage sprigs, about 6 leaves each

2 Tbsp. extra-virgin olive oil

¾ tsp. salt

¾ tsp. freshly ground pepper

1 To brine salmon: In a small saucepan, bring 4 cups water, maple syrup, ¼ cup salt, peppercorns, and bay leaf to a boil for 30 seconds. Remove from heat and cool to room temperature. Transfer the brine to a 2-gallon resealable plastic bag. Add the salmon and seal. Refrigerate, turning the bag occasionally to recoat the salmon, for 1 to 2 hours.

2 To make relish: Bring a small saucepan of water to a boil. Add ½ tsp. salt and corn; boil 1 minute. Drain the corn in a colander, rinsing under cold water until cool. In a medium bowl, combine the shallots and vinegar. Let stand 5 minutes. Drain the shallots and return to the bowl. Add the corn, red pepper, parsley, olive oil, sage, garlic, ground pepper, and remaining ½ tsp. salt. Refrigerate until ready to use.

3 To make the potatoes: Preheat the oven to 375°. In a large baking pan, combine the potatoes, garlic, sage, olive oil, salt, and pepper. Roast until the potatoes are tender, about 45 minutes.

4 Remove the salmon fillets from the brine and pat them dry with paper towels. Sprinkle both sides with the remaining ¼ tsp. salt. In 2 large skillets (preferably nonstick) over medium heat, add 1 Tbsp. canola oil to each and heat. Add 4 salmon fillets to each skillet, skin side up, and cook until opaque throughout (4 to 5 minutes per side). Serve with relish and potatoes.

Makes 8 servings.

147

Salmon Burgers

Chef: Laura Pensiero

A seasoned salmon patty tucked into a whole wheat bun adds up to a healthy fast food.

1 pound skinless wild salmon fillet
1 Tbsp. Dijon mustard
1 Tbsp. reduced-fat mayonnaise
1 Tbsp. chopped fresh chives
1 Tbsp. soy sauce
1 tsp. Asian sesame oil
¼ tsp. salt
⅛ tsp. freshly ground pepper
⅓ cup sesame seeds
2 tsp. peanut oil
4 whole wheat buns
4 tomato slices
1 ½ cups baby greens

1 Remove and discard any bones from salmon, then cut into 1-inch pieces. In a food processor, pulse salmon just until finely chopped (do not overprocess). Transfer salmon to a medium bowl. Add mustard, mayonnaise, chives, soy sauce, sesame oil, salt, and pepper; stir to combine. Form mixture into four 3½-inch patties. Generously sprinkle one side of each patty with sesame seeds.

2 Brush peanut oil over bottom of a large nonstick skillet to coat evenly. Place skillet over medium-high heat. Place burgers seed side down in skillet; cook until sesame seeds brown lightly, 2 to 3 minutes, reducing heat slightly, if necessary. With a spatula, gently turn burgers over and cook just until opaque in the center, about 3 minutes.

3 Transfer salmon burgers to buns, and top with tomato slices and greens.

Makes 4 burgers.

Cabbage-Wrapped Salmon Steamed in Wine

Chef: Art Smith

Who doesn't want to save the flavor and lose the fat? Here's one way to do it.

4 large cabbage leaves
Four (8-ounce) skinless salmon fillets
Salt and freshly ground pepper
1 medium carrot, cut into matchsticks
1 large leek, white part only, cut into
   matchsticks
1 small zucchini, cut into matchsticks
2 Roma (or plum) tomatoes, seeded
   and chopped
¼ cup minced shallots
2 Tbsp. chopped fresh parsley
1 Tbsp. chopped fresh tarragon
Kitchen string
2 cups white wine
1 lemon, quartered

1 In a large stockpot, bring 2 quarts of water to a boil. Blanch cabbage leaves for 1 to 2 minutes; set aside to cool.

2 Season salmon with salt and pepper and set aside.

3 In a large bowl, mix carrot, leek, zucchini, tomatoes, shallots, parsley, and tarragon; season lightly with salt and pepper. Place one salmon fillet in each cabbage leaf and surround it with several spoonfuls of seasoned vegetables. Gently fold cabbage around salmon and vegetables to create a packet. Tie closed with kitchen string.

4 In a large pot with a steaming basket insert, bring wine to a boil.

5 Place salmon packets in steaming basket; cook 5 minutes. Remove packets from pot, snip off kitchen string, and serve with lemon wedges.

Makes 4 servings.

Use a steaming basket, or, Art Smith suggests, pour a little water in a pan, crumple up some foil, and place the food on top.

"When I write a menu, I want to eat everything on it," says Govind Armstrong, the executive chef and owner of Table 8 in Los Angeles. Evidently, so do a lot of other people in town, who have made such a success of the restaurant that a branch of Table 8 recently opened on Miami's trendy South Beach.

Whether he is cooking at home or for diners in South Florida, Govind goes for an ingredient- and market-based cuisine that respects the seasons and local bounty. At least, he says, this is where he starts when developing one of his mouth-watering dishes.

The author of *Small Bites, Big Nights*, Govind begins at the same place when he writes recipes for the home cook. But, he says "I always think of how long the home cook has to spend in the kitchen, and I try to shave a few steps off the recipe."

"It's just *you* in the home kitchen," he says. "In the restaurant I have trained people to take care of so many different processes." For instance, when he calls for toasted walnuts and walnut oil in a recipe, he expects the home cook to buy shelled walnuts and bottled walnut oil. In the restaurant, one of the many sets of hands he has to help him will shell the nuts, toast them in oil, and then strain and use the walnut-infused oil to make a vinaigrette.

While Govind does not shy away from using canned foods for recipes meant for home cooking, he'll put his own spin on the ingredients. "I never use anything right out of the jar or can. I always add at least one last step," he says.

Adding extras defines his idea of Thanksgiving dinner, too. He says that like every American family, his gathers for the holiday feast and always has turkey. But, he says, there is always another protein on the table as well.

He started bringing duck to Thanksgiving dinner as an alternative to turkey and everyone loved it. It hasn't replaced the turkey, but it's a hit. "There's nothing I don't like about duck," Govind says. "It's so versatile."

Govind was born in Los Angeles, spent some years in Costa Rica, and then did most of his growing up in Encino, California, where his family tended a large garden full of corn, asparagus, broccoli, tomatoes, radishes, melons, strawberries, and herbs. Today, he maintains that this is how he developed an early connection with ingredient-based cooking. He credits his mother with igniting his fascination with cooking whatever was ripe and ready for consumption. "My mom loved to cook this way and she also loved to entertain," he remembers.

Govind laments he does not have much opportunity to cook and entertain at home these days, but with two successful restaurants on two different coasts, he is rarely away from the heat of the kitchen. When he is not there, he is making connections with local farmers, fishermen, and growers, so that he can make the ultimate connection: the one with the people who love his food.

> "I always think of how long the home cook has to spend in the kitchen, and I try to shave a few steps off the recipe."

Govind Armstrong's Recipes

- **Maple-Glazed Whole Duck with Savoy Cabbage** (page 128)
- **French Beans with Roasted Figs, Thyme, & Rustic Croutons** (page 165)
- **Candied Yams with Homemade Marshmallows** (page 189)
- **Fresh Cranberry Relish** (page 211)
- **Sweet Potato & Pecan Pie with Cinnamon Cream** (page 245)

Skewered Spicy Shrimp with Grilled Watermelon

Chef: Rori Trovato

Grilled watermelon? You have to try it to believe it.
When paired with shrimp, it's divine.

2 Tbsp. hot paprika

¼ tsp. cayenne pepper

1 tsp. kosher salt

1 ½ pounds large shrimp, peeled and deveined (about 36 shrimp)

2 Tbsp. olive oil

½ seedless watermelon, cut into quarters, then sliced into 1-inch-thick wedges

½ cup sugar

1 In a large bowl, combine paprika, cayenne, and salt. Add shrimp and toss until well coated. Cover and refrigerate 30 minutes.

2 Heat grill to medium-high. Divide shrimp among skewers, about 3 to each skewer. Brush with olive oil and grill 3 to 4 minutes each side, until pink and opaque.

3 Sprinkle one side of each watermelon wedge with sugar and place on the grill, sweetened side down, until sugar caramelizes, about 3 minutes (do not flip). Remove from grill. Top with skewered shrimp before serving.

Makes 4 servings.

Grilled Shrimp with Mango Salsa

Chef: Nina Simonds

This is an easy and appealing shrimp dish to make for company.
If there are any leftovers, serve them in a salad, stir-fry,
or as a garnish for butternut squash soup.

SALSA

2 large ripe mangoes, peeled, pitted, and diced

¼ cup minced red onion

¼ cup chopped cilantro leaves

3 Tbsp. fresh lime juice

1 tsp. minced fresh ginger

½ tsp. salt, or to taste

¼ tsp. freshly ground black pepper

SHRIMP

1 ½ pounds large shrimp, peeled and deveined

2 Tbsp. reduced-sodium soy sauce

2 Tbsp. fresh orange juice

2 Tbsp. olive oil, for grilling

1 To make salsa: Combine all ingredients in a bowl. Set aside.

2 To make shrimp: Rinse and drain shrimp; pat dry with paper towels. In a bowl, combine shrimp, soy sauce, and orange juice. Let stand 10 minutes.

3 Meanwhile, prepare a grill, oiling the grill rack. Thread shrimp onto metal skewers (or wooden skewers that have been soaked in water for about an hour). Brush with oil and grill over medium heat, regularly brushing with soy mixture, 3 to 4 minutes per side, until shrimp are cooked through. Remove from skewers and place on a serving platter. Serve with mango salsa, basmati rice, and Warm Roasted Vegetable Salad (page 36).

Makes about 6 servings, depending on size of shrimp.

"I love the combination of hot seafood and cold spicy fruit," Nina Simonds says of this recipe.

154

Grilled Shrimp with Mango Salsa and **Warm Roasted Vegetable Salad** (recipe on page 36)

Spicy Shrimp with Basil

Chef: Nina Simonds

The name says it all. Fresh and zingy, this easy stir-fry is a great meal.

MARINADE

3 Tbsp. rice wine
2 Tbsp. soy sauce
1 Tbsp. minced fresh ginger

1 ½ pounds medium shrimp, peeled and deveined
½ pound snow peas, trimmed

SEASONING

1 tsp. red pepper flakes
2 tsp. chopped garlic
2 medium red onions, julienned

SAUCE

3 Tbsp. Thai fish sauce
1 ½ Tbsp. soy sauce
1 Tbsp. sugar

2 ½ Tbsp. extra-virgin olive oil
1 ½ cups coarsely shredded fresh basil leaves

1 To make marinade: In a medium bowl, combine rice wine, 2 Tbsp. soy sauce, and ginger. Rinse shrimp and pat dry. With a sharp knife, score shrimp along the back to butterfly, then rinse and drain thoroughly. Add shrimp to the bowl and toss gently with marinade to coat. Refrigerate 20 minutes.

2 Meanwhile, in a saucepan, bring 1½ quarts water to a boil. Add snow peas and cook until crisp-tender, about 1½ minutes. Drain in a colander and refresh under cold water. Drain again.

3 To make seasoning: In a medium bowl, combine red pepper flakes, garlic, and red onion.

4 To make sauce: In a medium bowl, combine fish sauce, soy sauce, sugar, and 1½ Tbsp. water.

5 Heat a wok or a heavy skillet over high heat. Add 1 Tbsp. olive oil and heat until near smoking; swirl oil to coat the pan. Add shrimp and stir-fry until they change color and are just cooked, about 3 minutes. Drain shrimp; wipe out pan.

6 Add the remaining 1½ Tbsp. olive oil to pan and heat until very hot, about 30 seconds. Add seasoning mixture and stir-fry until onion is tender, about 3 minutes. Stir sauce and add to pan; bring to a boil. Stir in shrimp and basil. Transfer to a serving platter and serve with steamed rice, if desired.

Makes 6 servings.

Oprah's Favorite Crab Cakes

Adapted from The Polo Grill, Baltimore

Crab cakes don't get any better than these, which is no surprise considering they come from Maryland, where fresh crabs rule!

1 whole egg
2 tsp. lemon juice
¼ tsp. Worcestershire sauce
⅔ cup Hellman's mayonnaise
½ tsp. dry mustard
¼ tsp. celery seed
2 tsp. Old Bay seasoning
¼ tsp. salt
¼ tsp. pepper
1 pound fresh jumbo lump crabmeat
1 Tbsp. chopped flat-leaf parsley
2 Tbsp. bread crumbs, plus 1 ½ cups
   for coating

1 Preheat the oven to 425°. Whisk the egg in a bowl until blended. Stir in the lemon juice, Worcestershire sauce, and mayonnaise. In a separate bowl, mix the dry mustard, celery seed, Old Bay, salt, and pepper. Add the dry ingredients to the wet ones.

2 Remove any shell fragments from the crabmeat, then add the parsley and 2 Tbsp. of the bread crumbs. Gently mix with your fingers, taking care not to break too many of the jumbo lumps.

3 Gently fold the crab mixture into the wet mixture until blended. Form into 3-inch cakes and coat with remaining bread crumbs. Chill for 1 hour.

4 Place the cakes on a large greased cookie sheet and bake for 15 to 20 minutes, or until lightly browned on the outside, turning once with a metal spatula. Serve with cocktail sauce, tartar sauce, or simply a lemon.

Makes 4 crab cakes.

157

Grilled Sea Scallops with Tomato-Black Olive Vinaigrette & Potatoes

Created by Moira Hodgson

If you don't have a small-mesh grill rack, thread the scallops on skewers before grilling to prevent them from falling through the grid.

SCALLOPS

16 sea scallops (about 12 ounces), preferably diver caught*

3 Tbsp. extra-virgin olive oil

¾ tsp. salt

½ tsp. freshly ground black pepper

2 Tbsp. red wine vinegar, or to taste

1 garlic clove, finely chopped

3 to 4 large ripe tomatoes, seeded and chopped

¾ cup (about 4 ounces) oil-cured black olives, pitted and chopped

1 bunch basil, roughly chopped

POTATOES

4 large waxy potatoes (preferably Yukon Gold)

1 Tbsp. extra-virgin olive oil

½ tsp. salt

*Ask your purveyor for diver-caught scallops, which are gathered by hand and haven't been treated with phosphates, a practice that bloats scallops by up to 20 percent of their weight.

1 To make scallops: Rinse scallops and pat dry; place in a bowl. Season with 1 Tbsp. olive oil, ¼ tsp. salt, and ¼ tsp. pepper. Set aside.

2 In a mixing bowl, combine vinegar, remaining 2 Tbsp. olive oil, and garlic. Stir in tomatoes, olives, and basil. Season to taste with remaining ½ tsp. salt and ¼ tsp. pepper. Set aside. Preheat gas grill to medium-high, or prepare a charcoal grill for direct grilling over medium-high heat.

3 To make potatoes: Cut into slices about ⅓ inch thick. Steam on stovetop until barely tender, about 10 minutes. Transfer to a bowl, allow to cool slightly, and toss with olive oil and salt. Place potatoes on grill and cook 3 to 4 minutes per side, until browned. Remove to a serving platter and keep warm in a low oven.

4 Place scallops on grill fitted with an oiled, small-mesh grill rack and cook 1 minute per side, until edges are lightly browned. Divide scallops among 4 individual serving plates. Top with equal portions tomato-olive vinaigrette; serve with potatoes on the side.

Makes 4 servings.

158

Maine Lobster Acqua Pazza

Chef: Jody Williams

Lobster bathed in wine is insanely tasty.

One (2-pound) lobster*

3 Tbsp. extra-virgin olive oil, plus 2 tsp. for drizzling

3 garlic cloves, minced

Pinch of crushed red chilies

10 green olives, crushed and pitted

½ cup dry white wine

1 pint ripe cherry tomatoes, halved

6 fresh basil leaves

1 fresh mint sprig

¼ tsp. kosher salt

*When making this dish, start with a live lobster and a sharp knife, but if you're squeamish—or saw *Annie Hall* one too many times—you can ask your fishmonger to do the chopping for you and begin the recipe with step 2.

1 Start by cleaning lobster: With a heavy chef's knife, plunge tip straight down behind lobster's head. Cut lobster in half lengthwise, first through body cavity, then through tail section. Remove and discard stomach (the white sac located in lobster's head). Separate claws. With back of knife, crack claws and arms.

2 Place a large, heavy skillet over medium heat. Warm 3 Tbsp. olive oil and add lobster and its juices. Add garlic and chilies, cooking until golden brown. Add olives and cook 3 minutes, turning lobster occasionally.

3 Turn heat to high and add white wine and ¼ cup water. Reduce liquids 2 minutes. Add tomatoes, herbs, and salt and cook 1 to 2 minutes longer, or until lobster is cooked through. Cut into pieces and drizzle with olive oil. Serve with grilled Italian bread rubbed with garlic, if desired.

Makes 2 servings.

160

Celebration of Spring Vegetables
(recipe on page 164)

Chapter 7

VEGETABLE SIDE DISHES

Celebration of Spring Vegetables: English Peas, Favas, & Asparagus with Mint

Created by Peggy Knickerbocker

The delicate crunch of this dish makes eating your vegetables a pleasure.

1 ½ pounds fava beans, in shell
1 pound English peas, in shell
¾ pound yellow wax beans, trimmed
1 pound asparagus
4 Tbsp. extra-virgin olive oil, plus more
 for drizzling
1 medium onion, finely chopped
2 garlic cloves, minced
¼ cup dry white wine or water
Salt and freshly ground black pepper
½ cup mint chiffonade (see step 7)

1 While shelling fava beans, bring a small pot of water to a boil. Add shelled favas and cook 2 minutes. Drain, then plunge into ice water to stop cooking and set color. Drain again, then slip skin off each bean with your fingers. Place beans in a small bowl. Set aside.

2 Shell peas and add to favas. Meanwhile, in a saucepan, bring a few inches of water to a boil. Add wax beans and cook 2 minutes. Drain, then plunge into ice water. Drain again. Set aside.

3 Prepare asparagus by breaking tough ends off where they give, and then peel each stalk. Cut trimmed asparagus diagonally into 2-inch lengths. Set aside.

4 Warm 2 Tbsp. olive oil in a large skillet over medium-high heat. Add onion and cook until fragrant, about 2 minutes, stirring frequently. Add garlic and cook another minute or so, stirring frequently.

5 Add remaining 2 Tbsp. olive oil and asparagus, turn heat to medium-low, and cook until asparagus are just tender when pierced with a fork, 5 to 7 minutes, depending upon their thickness and freshness. Shake pan to prevent asparagus from sticking.

6 Add wax beans and stir to incorporate. Add wine or water and gently fold in favas and peas. Season with ¼ tsp. salt and ¼ tsp. pepper and cook just until favas and peas are warm, about 1 minute. Adjust seasoning, if necessary, before turning onto a warm serving platter. Scatter with mint chiffonade and drizzle with high-quality extra-virgin olive oil, if desired.

7 To make chiffonade: A chiffonade is the result of a slicing technique you can use on any leafy green or herb to produce feathery light strips. The technique is a neat and fast alternative to chopping, which often results in bruised and torn leaves. To make a mint chiffonade, stack 2 large mint leaves so that their spines are aligned. Gently roll them into a scroll-like tube. Hold one end of the tube with fingertips curled under, and with a sharp chef's knife in the other hand, slice mint crosswise, as thinly as possible. Fluff strips and use them as garnish or in salads.

Makes 4 to 6 servings.

French Beans with Roasted Figs, Thyme, & Rustic Croutons

Chef: Govind Armstrong

No fig leaf can hide the fact that figs are the sexiest fruit on earth, with sensuous curves on the outside and juicy, blushing flesh within.

CROUTONS

One (16-ounce) loaf walnut-raisin bread, crust removed, torn into bite-size pieces
2 Tbsp. walnut oil
¼ tsp. kosher salt
¼ tsp. freshly ground pepper

BEANS

3 pounds French green beans, ends trimmed
15 firm, ripe figs, cut in half lengthwise
10 large fresh thyme sprigs
2 Tbsp. balsamic vinegar
1 Tbsp. olive oil
¼ tsp. kosher salt
¼ tsp. freshly ground pepper

VINAIGRETTE

¼ cup sherry vinegar
2 ½ Tbsp. finely chopped walnuts, toasted
1 small shallot, minced
½ tsp. chopped fresh thyme leaves
½ tsp. kosher salt
½ tsp. freshly ground pepper
¼ cup walnut oil
¼ cup olive oil

1 small bunch flat-leaf parsley, stems removed

1 To make croutons: Preheat oven to 375°. On a baking sheet with sides, toss pieces of bread with walnut oil, salt, and pepper. Bake 10 minutes, tossing once or twice, or until browned and crisp. Let cool. Leave oven on.

2 To make beans: Bring a large pot of salted water to a boil; add green beans. Cook 4 minutes, or until bright green and slightly tender; drain. Refresh under cold water; drain again and pat dry with paper towels.

3 In a medium bowl, gently toss figs with thyme sprigs, vinegar, olive oil, salt, and pepper. On a baking sheet with sides, lay figs, cut side down, and roast 10 minutes, or until lightly caramelized and cooked through. Cool on baking sheet.

4 To make vinaigrette: In a medium bowl, whisk vinegar, walnuts, shallot, chopped thyme, salt, and pepper; gradually whisk in walnut and olive oils until blended.

5 In a large bowl, toss croutons, green beans, and parsley leaves with vinaigrette. Arrange on plates, and top each with 3 roasted fig halves.

Makes 10 servings.

Braised Fennel with Onions & Balsamic Vinegar

Chef: Colin Cowie

Fennel is a gem of the vegetable kingdom, and braising accentuates its anise-like flavor.

3 Tbsp. olive oil
8 ounces (2 cups) pearl onions, peeled
3 large fennel bulbs (about 2¼ pounds), ends trimmed, cored and thinly sliced lengthwise
1 Tbsp. minced garlic
1 cup chicken broth
2 bay leaves
½ tsp. salt
¼ tsp. ground black pepper
1 Tbsp. chopped fresh marjoram or oregano leaves
1 to 2 Tbsp. balsamic vinegar

1 Heat oil in large deep skillet over medium heat. Add onions and cook, stirring, until browned, 5 minutes. Add fennel and garlic; cook, stirring occasionally, until fennel begins to soften, 5 minutes.

2 Add broth, bay leaves, salt, and pepper. Bring to a simmer, reduce heat to medium-low, and cook, covered, until the fennel is tender-crisp, 10 minutes.

3 Increase heat to high, and cook until almost all of the liquid is evaporated, 3 to 5 minutes. Remove bay leaves. Stir in marjoram and vinegar; cook 1 minute, or until flavored through.

Makes 10 servings.

166

Poppy Seed–Crusted Cauliflower

Chef: Colin Cowie

With one bite of this Indian-inspired dish, you'll
develop a new appreciation for cauliflower.

5 Tbsp. black or white poppy seeds*

6 or 7 small dried hot red chilies, like
Japone or Thai (3 stemmed, seeded,
and broken into pieces, and 3 or 4
whole)

½ tsp. ground turmeric

1 tsp. salt

1 tsp. sugar

1 medium-size cauliflower (about 2
pounds), cut into ½-inch florets

3 Tbsp. vegetable oil

½ tsp. nigella seeds*

2 bay leaves

*White poppy seeds and nigella
seeds (also known as kalonji or
black onion seeds) are available
at www.kalustyans.com.

1 Grind poppy seeds and chili
pieces in a spice or coffee grinder
until they form a fine powder; transfer to a small bowl and mix with 6
Tbsp. water to form a paste. Set aside.

2 In a medium bowl, combine
turmeric, ½ tsp. salt, and ½ tsp.
sugar; add cauliflower and toss
until evenly coated. Set aside.

3 In a large nonstick skillet, heat
2 Tbsp. oil over medium-high
heat. When oil is hot, add cauliflower and stir-fry 4 to 6 minutes,
until it begins to brown in spots;
remove with slotted spoon to baking sheet lined with paper towels.

4 Add remaining 1 Tbsp. oil to
skillet over medium heat.
When oil is hot, add nigella seeds,
bay leaves, and whole chilies. Stir-fry 15 seconds, then add poppy
seed paste. Stir-fry 1 to 2 minutes,
until fragrant; stir in cauliflower
and remaining ½ tsp. each salt and
sugar until cauliflower is coated.

5 Add ⅔ cup water; bring to a
boil. Cover, reduce heat to low,
and simmer 4 to 6 minutes, stirring
once or twice, until cauliflower is
just tender and sauce is absorbed.

Makes 6 servings.

Roasted Carrots, Pearl Onions, & Wild Mushrooms with Tarragon

Chef: Govind Armstrong

Mastering simple cooking techniques, like high-heat roasting, opens up a world of mealtime options. These roasted vegetables are irresistible.

1 ½ pounds pearl onions
Two (1-pound) bags baby carrots
16 large thyme sprigs
2 Tbsp. extra-virgin olive oil
1 ¼ tsp. kosher salt
¾ tsp. freshly ground pepper
8 ounces mixed wild mushrooms
  (cremini, shiitake, and oyster)
2 Tbsp. butter
½ cup chicken broth
2 Tbsp. sherry vinegar
2 Tbsp. coarsely chopped fresh
  tarragon leaves

1 Bring a large pot of salted water to a boil; add onions. Blanch 2 minutes; drain in a colander and let cool. Trim stem and root ends, then slip onions out of their skins.

2 Preheat oven to 450°. Place onions and carrots each on a separate baking sheet with sides. To each sheet, add 8 thyme sprigs, 1 Tbsp. olive oil, ½ tsp. salt, and ¼ tsp. pepper; toss until vegetables are coated evenly. Roast 25 minutes, tossing vegetables several times until lightly caramelized and slightly tender; cool.

3 Quarter cremini mushrooms; remove stems from shiitake mushrooms and slice caps; slice oyster mushrooms. In a large, deep skillet over high heat, melt butter and sauté mushrooms until tender, about 4 minutes. Add roasted onions, carrots, broth, and vinegar. Cook, tossing vegetables with a large spoon, until broth and vinegar have evaporated and vegetables are heated through, 3 to 4 minutes. Add tarragon and remaining ¼ tsp. salt and ¼ tsp. pepper; toss.

Makes 10 servings.

168

Roasted Beets with Ginger

Chef: Nina Simonds

Fresh beets are incredibly sweet and tender and, when roasted with ginger, are even more spectacular.

2 Tbsp. extra-virgin olive oil
1 ½ Tbsp. minced fresh ginger
2 ½ Tbsp. balsamic vinegar
2 ½ pounds medium-size fresh beets, stems trimmed to 1 inch

1 Preheat oven to 450°. Line a cookie sheet with foil.

2 In a small bowl, combine olive oil, ginger, and vinegar.

3 Cut beets in half and arrange, cut side up, on cookie sheet.

Brush all parts of beets except the stems with ginger-vinegar mixture. Roast, uncovered, until beets are very tender, 20 to 25 minutes. Arrange on a platter, cool slightly, and serve warm.

Makes 6 servings.

Broiled Asparagus with Miso & Ginger

Chef: Rori Trovato

Asparagus with miso delivers a study in contrasts: delicate stalks with a shot of a tangy, exotic, and potent sauce. A knockout!

¼ cup miso paste
1 small clove garlic, minced
1 tsp. minced fresh ginger
2 tsp. fresh lime juice
1 pinch red pepper flakes
1 Tbsp. boiling water
1 ½ pounds asparagus, bottoms trimmed
1 Tbsp. olive oil
Pinch of salt

1 Preheat broiler. In a medium bowl, combine miso paste with garlic, ginger, lime juice, pepper flakes, and water. Stir well and set aside.

2 Toss asparagus with olive oil and salt. Place on a baking sheet and set on a rack 6 inches from broiler. Broil 3 minutes, then remove from heat. Toss asparagus with miso mixture and place back under broiler. Broil until tender and slightly charred, 3 to 5 minutes.

Makes 4 servings.

Roasted Beets with Ginger

At the Table with Nina Simonds
THE STORY OF A FAST EATER

"The family is where it's at in Asian culture," says Nina Simonds, who is known as one of the foremost authorities on Asian cooking and culinary traditions. "Whenever and wherever I visit in Asia, I always find an emphasis on family, and it's this dedication to it that I brought home with me after living there the first time."

Nina recalls that when she was a child, her parents' evening ritual included watching the nightly news, so she and her sister and two brothers frequently gobbled up their food in the ten minutes before the news came on and her mother and father abandoned the table for the living room sofa. "My husband couldn't believe what a fast eater I was when he first met me," she says with a laugh. Things changed when she went to live in Taiwan in the early 1970s at the age of 19. She was a serious student of food, language, and culture, and to learn as much as she could, she lived in a Taiwanese household. She quickly adopted her hosts as a surrogate family. They, in turn, joyfully embraced their Western daughter.

"Every morning, we went to the market to pick out food for two or three dinners," Nina remembers. "Dinner was one of the most important parts of the day because it was a time when the entire family gathered. Everyone stopped what they were doing and sat down at a large round table with a Lazy Susan in the middle. There were always two vegetables, a little meat, and sometimes a little fish. And there was always a simple soup and steamed rice."

The scarcity of meat had nothing to do with the family's income—they were well off—and everything to

> "Whenever and wherever I visit in Asia, I always find an emphasis on family, and it's this dedication to it that I brought home with me after living there the first time."

do with how the Chinese and most other Asian cultures assemble a meal.

Nina explains that everyone took food from the communal bowls and ate it with the rice. When your rice bowl was empty, she says, you filled it with what was left of the soup to drink as an aid to digestion.

The author of ten books on Chinese cuisine and culture, including the best-selling *Asian Noodles* and *A Spoonful of Ginger*, Nina still travels to Asia at least once a year and dreams of spending a year or two living in Shanghai. Today, she wanders far from the cultural and urban centers in search of authentic food and customs that have not been influenced by the West. "It's sad to see how Asians have adopted some of our Western customs," she says. "On the other hand, I also see them coming full circle and re-adopting their own traditions for a more healthful life—things like less meat and more grains and vegetables at a meal."

But regardless of what she finds in Asian cities or small hamlets, she is always drawn to the value of the family she finds everywhere. "The richness of sharing these customs is what it's all about," she concludes.

Nina Simond's Recipes
- **Warm Roasted Vegetable Salad** (page 36)
- **Sautéed Chicken with Cherry Tomatoes** (page 115)
- **Grilled Shrimp with Mango Salsa** (page 154)
- **Spicy Shrimp with Basil** (page 156)
- **Roasted Beets with Ginger** (page 170)
- **Pumpkin Applesauce Muffins** (page 230)

Sautéed Swiss Chard

Chef: Mollie Ahlstrand

Chard is simply glorious when sautéed with a few well-chosen ingredients.

1 ½ pounds Swiss chard
1 Tbsp. plus ¼ tsp. salt
1 Tbsp. extra-virgin olive oil
½ cup chopped onion
⅓ cup chopped shallot
2 cloves garlic, finely chopped
½ tsp. red pepper flakes
1 cup tomato sauce

1 In a large pot, bring 3 quarts water to a boil. Snip chard stems and reserve.

2 When water reaches a boil, add 1 Tbsp. salt. Add stems; cover and cook 3 minutes (begin timing as soon as stems are added). Add leaves; cover and cook 5 more minutes. Drain in colander; rinse under cold water until cool. Drain again, squeezing to remove any excess liquid. Coarsely chop.

3 In a large skillet, heat oil over medium-high heat. Add onion, shallot, and garlic; cook, stirring, until golden, about 2 minutes. Stir in red pepper flakes. Add chard and tomato sauce; reduce heat to medium and cook 5 minutes. Stir in ¼ tsp. salt.

Makes 6 servings.

Garlic-Orange Spinach

Chef: Michel Nischan

The spinach blends beautifully with the garlic and orange juice.

2 Tbsp. grapeseed or rice oil
1 Tbsp. thinly sliced garlic
3 Tbsp. freshly squeezed orange juice
One (10-ounce) bag fresh spinach leaves, stems removed, washed and spun dry
1 Tbsp. grated orange zest
Sea salt and freshly ground pepper

In a large sauté pan, heat oil over medium-high heat. Add garlic and cook, stirring constantly, until it begins to brown, about 30 seconds. Add orange juice and cook until reduced, about 30 seconds. Add spinach and orange zest; sauté until spinach just wilts. Remove from heat and season with salt and pepper.

Makes 4 servings.

Stuffed Acorn Squash

Chef: Daniel Boulud

The bacon-wrapped squash and mushroom-chard filling are almost decadent—and the squash can be prepared a day ahead, which makes it perfect for a party.

3 medium acorn squash (about 2½ pounds each)

5 Tbsp. extra-virgin olive oil, divided

Salt and freshly ground pepper

12 slices bacon

1 medium onion, peeled and finely chopped

2 garlic cloves, peeled and crushed

2 ½ pounds Swiss chard, washed, dried, and stems and center veins removed

10 ounces assorted mushrooms (such as chanterelles, oyster, white, cremini), trimmed

1 tsp. finely chopped thyme leaves

⅛ tsp. freshly grated nutmeg

¼ cup dried bread crumbs

1 Tbsp. finely chopped Italian parsley

1 Tbsp. butter, melted

1 Preheat oven to 375°. Soak about 30 rounded wooden toothpicks in warm water.

2 Using a sharp knife, slice off a little of the squash bottoms so they sit flat. Turn squash on their sides and cut off tops (about 1 inch), exposing the seeds. Turn squash over, seed side down. With a sharp knife, completely slice away green peel, following the curve of the squash. Use a big spoon to scoop out and discard seeds and membrane. Brush squash with 1 Tbsp. olive oil, and season inside and out with salt and freshly ground pepper to taste.

3 Working with one squash at a time, wrap 4 slices of bacon around each so they resemble the spokes of a wheel, tucking one end of each strip under the squash and securing the other end inside the rim with a toothpick. Place a rack in the bottom of a large, shallow baking dish. Arrange squash, hollow side down, on rack. Bake on center oven rack 30 minutes—basting every 10 minutes with pan juices—until bacon is browned and squash is nearly tender when pierced with a knife. Remove from oven and set aside to cool.

4 Warm 2 Tbsp. olive oil in a large, preferably nonstick, skillet over medium heat. Add onion and garlic. Cook, stirring frequently, 5 to 7 minutes, until onion is soft. Increase heat to medium-high and start adding chard in big batches. As greens wilt, transfer to a plate and add more chard to pan until it is all wilted. Return all chard to pan and cook until tender yet still quite green. Transfer to a plate to cool; discard garlic cloves.

5 Wipe pan with paper towel and place over medium-high heat. Add remaining 2 Tbsp. olive oil and mushrooms. Stir until mushrooms are tender and no liquid is left in pan. Transfer to a plate to cool. When chard is cool enough to handle, squeeze out excess juice.

Toss chard with mushrooms; add thyme and nutmeg. Season with salt and pepper to taste.

6 Preheat oven to 500°. Mix together bread crumbs, parsley, and melted butter, and season with salt and pepper to taste. Remove toothpicks from squash and turn them right side up in the baking dish. Stuff squash with chard mixture so it's packed and creates a small mound. Sprinkle an equal amount of bread crumbs on top of each squash. Bake 10 minutes on center oven rack, until crust is golden brown and squash are heated through. Transfer to cutting board and let rest 5 minutes. Use a sharp knife to cut each squash into 4 wedges (between bacon slices).

Makes 12 servings.

Grilled Vegetables with Lemon & Herbs

Created by Moira Hodgson

Eggplant, zucchini, and peppers are just the ticket for a summertime meal.

1 large (or 2 baby) eggplant

Sea salt

4 zucchini or yellow squash (or any combination of the two)

1 red bell pepper

1 yellow bell pepper

⅔ cup olive oil, divided

1 garlic clove, peeled

3 Tbsp. fresh lemon juice (about 1 lemon)

½ cup chopped fresh herbs (such as basil, marjoram, thyme, chives, flat-leaf parsley, or any combination of the five)

Freshly ground pepper to taste

1 Cut eggplant into ⅓-inch-thick slices. (If using baby eggplant, cut in half lengthwise and score flesh about ¼ inch deep in a criss-cross pattern with a knife.) Sprinkle eggplant with 1 tsp. salt, and let drain in a colander 30 minutes. Pat dry with paper towels.

2 Meanwhile, preheat grill to medium heat (if using grill pan on stovetop, heat to medium-high). Cut zucchini and/or yellow squash lengthwise into ¼-inch slices. Cut peppers in half and remove seeds and stems.

3 Grill peppers, skin side down. When skins have blackened and blistered, put peppers in a paper or plastic bag and close it. Allow peppers to cool, then slip off their skins with your fingers.

4 Brush zucchini and eggplant with ⅓ cup olive oil. Grill in batches, about 5 minutes on each side. (Take care not to burn eggplant, but make sure it is fully cooked.) Arrange cooked vegetables on a platter with peppers.

5 Chop garlic and, using a mortar and pestle or the tines of a fork on a plate, mash it with ½ tsp. salt. Place mixture in a small bowl. Add lemon juice, then mix in remaining ⅓ cup olive oil.

6 Drizzle vegetables with dressing. Sprinkle with herbs and salt and pepper to taste. Cover with a sheet of foil, and set aside until ready to serve. Do not refrigerate.

Makes 4 servings.

Brussels Sprouts with Chestnuts & Honey Mustard Dressing

Chef: April Bloomfield

Brussels sprouts with a bold dressing are downright delicious.

DRESSING

3 lemons
1 cup extra-virgin olive oil
3 Tbsp. Dijon mustard
2 Tbsp. chestnut honey
1 Tbsp. whole grain mustard
1 tsp. chopped fresh thyme leaves
1 tsp. kosher salt
½ tsp. freshly ground pepper

VEGETABLES

½ pound fresh chestnuts
2 containers (10 ounces each) fresh brussels sprouts, trimmed
8 Tbsp. (1 stick) unsalted butter
Kosher salt and freshly ground pepper

1 To make dressing: In a small saucepan, cover 1 lemon with water. Bring to a boil; reduce heat and simmer until soft, about an hour, turning lemon occasionally. Remove lemon and let cool. Cut lemon in half and with a teaspoon scrape out pulp, leaving just the peel; finely chop peel. Squeeze 4 Tbsp. juice from remaining lemons. In a bowl, mix lemon peel, olive oil, Dijon mustard, honey, whole grain mustard, thyme, salt, and pepper. Whisk to combine.

2 To prepare vegetables: With a paring knife, cut an X in the flat side of each chestnut shell. In a saucepan, cover chestnuts with water and bring to a boil; reduce heat and simmer until tender, about 15 minutes. Drain chestnuts. When cool enough to handle but still warm, peel chestnuts.

3 With tip of paring knife, make a shallow X in the bottom of each brussels sprout. Bring a large pot of salted water to a boil. Add brussels sprouts and cook until tender, about 6 minutes. Drain and run under cold water until cool.

4 In a large skillet, melt butter over medium heat. Add chestnuts and sprouts; season with salt and pepper to taste. Cook, turning occasionally with a spatula, until vegetables are browned, 15 to 20 minutes. With a slotted spoon, remove vegetables to a large serving platter. Whisk dressing and drizzle ¼ cup over vegetables.

Makes 8 servings.

177

Turnips & Broccoli Rabe with Parsley

Chef: April Bloomfield

Turnips often are overlooked, but their deep earthiness brings body and flavor to this lovely autumn dish.

4 medium turnips (about 1¼ pounds)
¾ pound turnip greens
2 bunches broccoli rabe (2 pounds), trimmed
4 Tbsp. olive oil, plus additional to taste
3 large garlic cloves, minced
¼ cup chopped flat-leaf parsley
1 tsp. ground fennel seeds
1 tsp. sea salt
¼ tsp. freshly ground pepper

1 Bring a pot of salted water to a boil. Cut each turnip into 4 wedges and add to boiling water; cook until just tender, about 10 minutes; drain. When turnips are cool enough to handle, peel and coarsely chop.

2 Bring a second pot of salted water to a boil. Add turnip greens and cook until just tender, about 5 minutes. Remove with a slotted spoon to a colander and let drain. Repeat with broccoli rabe. Reserve ½ cup cooking liquid. Let greens cool and then roughly chop.

3 In a large, deep skillet, heat 4 Tbsp. olive oil over medium heat. Add garlic, parsley, and ground fennel seeds. Cook, stirring constantly, until garlic begins to brown, about 30 seconds. Add turnips, greens, salt, and pepper. Cook, stirring frequently, until greens are tender and begin to stick to skillet, about 10 minutes. Add some reserved cooking liquid to moisten. Turn heat to low and let stand 2 minutes. Drizzle with additional olive oil if desired. Turn greens out onto a platter to serve.

Makes 8 servings.

Caramelized Onion & Bacon Tart

Chef: Susan Spungen

Chances are you already have everything you need in
your pantry for this wonderfully rich tart.

4 slices bacon, cut into ½-inch pieces

4 small onions, cut in half lengthwise
and thickly sliced

1 Tbsp. plus 1 tsp. chopped fresh thyme
leaves

Kosher salt

1 cup whole-milk ricotta cheese

1 egg yolk

Freshly ground pepper

¼ cup plus 1 Tbsp. Parmigiano-
Reggiano

One (8-inch) frozen pie or tart shell

1 Preheat oven to 350°. Cook bacon in a medium frying pan over medium-high heat until fat is mostly rendered and bacon is crisp around edges. Transfer to paper towels to drain, and set aside, leaving 1 Tbsp. bacon fat in pan. Crumble bacon after cooling.

2 Add onions to pan and cook over medium-high heat, stirring occasionally, until they start to brown, about 8 minutes. Turn heat to medium-low and add 1 Tbsp. thyme and pinch of salt. Continue to cook until onions are soft and deep golden brown, about 20 minutes more.

3 Meanwhile, combine ricotta, egg yolk, ½ tsp. salt, pinch of pepper, 1 tsp. thyme, and ¼ cup Parmigiano in a small bowl. Stir well to combine.

4 Spread ricotta mixture evenly on the bottom of tart shell. Arrange onions on top of ricotta and sprinkle with 1 Tbsp. Parmigiano. Sprinkle bacon over top. Transfer to oven and bake until edges of filling are golden brown, 30 to 40 minutes.

Makes 6 to 8 servings.

Mango Couscous
(recipe on page 202)

Chapter 8

POTATOES, PASTA, & GRAINS

Steamed Fingerling Potatoes with Crème Fraîche

Chef: Suzanne Goin

Half the potatoes are left whole, the other half mashed. Both are topped with crème frâiche and snipped chives.

2 pounds tiny fingerling potatoes, well scrubbed

2 Tbsp. butter

2 Tbsp. crème fraîche, plus additional, for garnish

1 tsp. fleur de sel or kosher salt

½ tsp. cracked black pepper

1 Tbsp. coarsely chopped basil, preferably opal

1 Tbsp. minced chives, plus several whole, for garnish

1 Place potatoes in a steamer basket over 1 inch simmering water. Cover and steam until tender, 15 to 20 minutes.

2 In a saucepan, mash half of the potatoes with a potato masher. Add remaining potatoes, butter, crème fraîche, fleur de sel, and pepper. Gently stir to combine.

3 Transfer potatoes to a serving bowl. Garnish with crème fraîche, basil, and chives.

Makes 6 servings.

184

Salt-Roasted Yukon Gold Potatoes with Bay Leaves

Chef: Rori Trovato

Potatoes, salt, olive oil—what could be more ordinary? But when the potatoes are buttery Yukon Golds, the salt is sea salt, and the oil is extra-virgin, this root vegetable takes flight.

4 Yukon Gold potatoes (1½ to 2 pounds), scrubbed

16 bay leaves, halved lengthwise

2 garlic cloves, cut into thin slivers

1 cup coarse sea salt

3 Tbsp. extra-virgin olive oil

1 Preheat oven to 450°. Using a paring knife, make 8 tiny slits on top of each potato, about ¾ inch deep and just wide enough to fit a bay leaf and garlic sliver. Place bay leaves and garlic slivers into slits. Sprinkle with 2 tsp. sea salt. Spread remaining sea salt on a 9-inch-square pan. Place potatoes on top and roast until tender, about 1 hour.

2 Remove potatoes from oven and drizzle with olive oil. Discard bay leaves before eating.

Makes 4 servings.

Steamed Fingerling Potatoes
with Crème Fraîche

Two-Potato Gratin

Chef: Paula Disbrowe

Sweet or savory, a dish made with potatoes is just the most delicious part of any meal. Heavy on the starch, please.

1 Tbsp. butter

1 cup whole or 2 percent milk, cream, or half-and-half

¾ tsp. salt

⅛ tsp. freshly ground pepper

Pinch of ancho chili powder

Pinch of grated nutmeg

1 pound Yukon Gold potatoes, peeled and sliced into ½-inch-thick rounds

1 pound sweet potatoes, peeled and sliced into ½-inch-thick rounds

3 Tbsp. whole grain mustard

1 cup shredded Gruyère cheese

1 Preheat oven to 400°. Butter a shallow 2-quart gratin pan or ceramic baking dish.

2 In a large saucepan, combine milk, salt, pepper, chili powder, and nutmeg. Heat to boiling over medium-high heat. Add potatoes and return to a boil; simmer a few minutes, until mixture thickens slightly. Remove pan from heat; stir in mustard.

3 With a slotted spoon, transfer half the potatoes to gratin dish; place in an even layer. Sprinkle with ½ cup Gruyère. Top with remaining potatoes; pour milk mixture over potatoes and sprinkle with remaining ½ cup Gruyère. Bake 40 minutes, until potatoes are tender and top is golden.

Serves 6.

186

Marcus Samuelsson, arguably one of the most talented and celebrated chefs of our time, is a star in the global culinary firmament. An exacting cook, Marcus takes time with all the dishes he creates. He may be satisfied with the flavor, but five other qualities must fall in line before he signs off on the final product: quality, texture, aesthetics, temperature, and top-notch raw materials.

Marcus first came to the United States in 1991 as a young apprentice for New York City's renowned Aquavit, and then left after his designated eight-month stint to cook in France at the famed restaurant Georges Blanc in Lyons. He returned to Aquavit in 1994 and has never left. A short time after his return, he became the youngest chef to earn three stars from the *New York Times,* and the accolades just keep coming.

"The concept for a restaurant is the chef's journey and philosophy," he explains. "All chefs have different means for developing a dish. For me, it could start with something I tasted on a trip or else I might just get creative with a familiar dish. Some recipes start with a foundation, for example, plain couscous. Then you build on the dish by adding spices, fruit, or meat until you are satisfied with your creation."

His own journey has been fascinating. Born in Ethiopia, he and his sister were adopted by a Swedish couple when Marcus was only three years old. He describes his Swedish childhood as idyllic and, when he was a teenager, his serious study of the culinary arts led him to other European countries before he finally landed in the United States. Today, he cooks sophisticated food rooted in the traditional and contemporary gastronomy of Scandinavia.

Now he is turning his attention with increasing frequency to the continent of his birth. His book, *The Soul of a New Cuisine: A Discovery of the Foods and Flavors of Africa*, has a foreword by Archbishop Desmond Tutu, and Marcus says he hopes that Americans will come to see the link between American and African food.

"We only hear about war and famine in Africa," he says sadly. "But it has proud, fantastic food."

Whether he is discussing various European or African cuisines, or the cooking of the United States, he sees food as an opportunity to enlighten others. When he comes up with recipes, he tries to make sure they "reveal a sense of my culture and a sense of my restaurant."

He urges home cooks to pay attention to the right tools (how can you slice salmon very thin if you don't have a sharp, flexible knife?), the temperature of the heat under the pots, and the temperature of the food when it is put on the table. He also advises home cooks to pay attention to the aesthetics of serving and eating the food, with a well-set table and good lighting as the place to start.

> "All chefs have different means for developing a dish. For me, it could start with something I tasted on a trip."

Marcus Samuelsson's Recipes

- **Callaloo** (page 74)
- **Lemon-Olive Chicken with Vegetable Tagine** (page 116)
- **Mango Couscous** (page 202)
- **Beet-Ginger Chutney** (page 213)

Candied Yams with Homemade Marshmallows

Chef: Govind Armstrong

When you make your own marshmallows, the yams are even more yummy.
Of course, a ten-ounce bag of store-bought works, too.

MARSHMALLOWS

1 Tbsp. grapeseed or vegetable oil
Confectioners' sugar, for dusting (about 1 cup)
2 envelopes unflavored gelatin
1 ½ cups granulated sugar
½ cup light corn syrup
1 tsp. vanilla extract

YAMS

5 pounds medium-size garnet yams or sweet potatoes
1 ¼ cups graham cracker crumbs
½ cup toasted walnuts
1 Tbsp. firmly packed brown sugar
¼ cup butter, melted

1 To make marshmallows: Brush a 9-inch-square pan with oil. Generously dust with confectioners' sugar, tapping out excess. In the large bowl of an electric mixer, pour ½ cup water. Sprinkle gelatin on top; let stand until gelatin softens, about 5 minutes.

2 In a small saucepan over medium-low heat, combine granulated sugar, corn syrup, and 3 Tbsp. water. Bring to a boil, stirring to dissolve sugar. Continue boiling, without stirring, until syrup reaches 240° (soft-ball stage) on a candy thermometer. Immediately remove pan from heat.

3 Using the whisk attachment of a mixer, beat gelatin mixture at high speed. Gradually add hot syrup in a thin, steady stream. Beat 5 minutes longer, until mixture is white, fluffy, and stiff. Beat in vanilla. Pour marshmallow mixture into prepared pan. Using a spatula brushed with oil, spread marshmallow evenly in pan. Let stand uncovered at room temperature 10 to 12 hours.

4 Dust a large cutting board with confectioners' sugar. Brush a knife with oil, then cut around marshmallow edges to loosen from pan. Cut marshmallow into quarters. Using a spatula brushed with oil, transfer pieces to the cutting board. Cut marshmallow quarters into 1-inch squares.

5 To make yams: Preheat oven to 400°. Place yams on a baking sheet; roast 50 to 60 minutes, or until fork-tender. Let cool completely. Peel yams, cut into 1-inch squares, and set aside.

6 Reduce oven temperature to 350°. In a food processor, combine graham cracker crumbs, walnuts, and brown sugar until nuts are finely ground. Transfer to a bowl, add butter, and toss with a fork until crumbs are evenly moistened. Press crumbs onto bottom of a 13" x 9" x 2" glass dish. Arrange yams on crust. Top evenly with marshmallows. Bake until marshmallows are melted and browned on top, 25 to 30 minutes.

Makes 10 servings.

189

Spaghetti al Limone

Created by Moira Hodgson

Some of the best pasta dishes are the simplest. This one falls into that category; it's really easy and really good.

1 pound spaghetti

1 ½ cups freshly grated Parmigiano-Reggiano cheese

¾ cup fresh lemon juice (3 to 4 lemons)

⅔ cup extra-virgin olive oil

½ tsp. sea salt

½ tsp. freshly ground pepper

2 tsp. grated lemon zest

2 cups slivered firmly packed basil leaves

1 In a large pot, cook spaghetti in salted, boiling water until al dente. Place a colander over a large serving bowl, then drain spaghetti into it (hot water will warm bowl). Pour water from bowl, wipe bowl dry, then empty spaghetti into it.

2 Meanwhile, combine cheese and lemon juice in a small mixing bowl. Gradually beat in olive oil until mixture becomes thick and creamy and cheese "melts" into oil. Season with salt and pepper. Stir in lemon zest.

3 Pour sauce over cooked spaghetti in serving bowl; toss thoroughly. Add basil, toss again, and serve.

Makes 6 servings.

Gnocchi with Fall Sage Pesto

Chef: Rori Trovato

Made from potatoes, gnocchi are a little labor intensive but well worth the effort.
The sage pesto is absolutely fabulous and quite unexpected.

GNOCCHI

2 ½ pounds large russet potatoes, scrubbed

2 Tbsp. plus 1 tsp. salt

1 ½ to 2 cups all-purpose flour

PESTO

⅓ cup minced fresh parsley

2 Tbsp. minced fresh sage

1 Tbsp. minced fresh rosemary

1 garlic clove, peeled

½ cup extra-virgin olive oil

2 Tbsp. toasted pine nuts

¼ to ½ cup grated Parmesan cheese

Salt and freshly ground pepper

1 Preheat oven to 450°. Pierce potatoes twice with a knife just deep enough to break the skin. Bake potatoes 1 hour, or until very tender. While potatoes are still hot, scoop out flesh from skins. Push through a ricer (best for lump-free potatoes) into a large bowl or mash by hand; add 1 tsp. salt. Knead in flour, starting with 1½ cups. If dough is not sticky, no additional flour is needed. If sticky, add more flour, 1 Tbsp. at a time. Gently press dough into ball; divide in half.

2 On a floured surface, with floured hands, knead each half until smooth. Divide each piece into 6 equal parts. Roll each segment into a rope, about ½ inch in diameter. Cut each rope into ¾-inch lengths.

3 Place one piece of dough on inside curve of fork tines, gently pressing with thumb as you roll dough along tines. Allow dough to drop off fork. (One side of gnocchi will have ridges; opposite side will have an indentation.) Repeat shaping with remaining dough. Place gnocchi on a baking sheet lined with parchment or waxed paper, and sift flour on top. (Gnocchi can be left out several hours or uncovered in refrigerator overnight.)

4 To make pesto: In a food processor or blender, mix herbs and garlic until smooth. Slowly add olive oil, scraping down sides of bowl. Add pine nuts and enough cheese to thicken. Season with salt and pepper. Set aside.

5 Meanwhile, bring a large pot of water to a boil with 2 Tbsp. salt. When water is rapidly boiling, carefully add gnocchi. After 3 to 5 minutes (gnocchi should begin to float), test one to make sure it's cooked through. Remove with a slotted spoon and place in a warm bowl. Thin pesto with ⅓ cup cooking water, adding more as necessary (pesto should have consistency of heavy cream), and pour over gnocchi in bowl. Toss carefully and serve with additional Parmesan, if desired.

Makes 4 to 6 servings.

Bolognese Sauce with Pasta

Created by Celia Barbour

This rich, meaty sauce simmers for hours, with spectacular results.

1 medium onion

1 large or 2 small carrots

2 to 3 celery stalks

1 ounce pancetta, very finely chopped

1 pound ground beef (not lean)

1 tsp. salt

1/8 tsp. freshly ground pepper

Pinch of allspice

1 cup whole milk

1 cup dry white wine

One (15-ounce) can diced tomatoes with their juice

1 pound pasta, such as rigatoni

Parmigiano-Reggiano cheese, for grating

1 Finely chop onion, carrot, and celery. In a heavy-bottomed saucepan or Dutch oven over low heat, cook pancetta until all fat is rendered and pancetta is just beginning to brown. Add chopped vegetables, raise heat to medium, and cook, stirring frequently, until onion is translucent and soft.

2 Add ground beef, breaking it up with a spoon, ¼ tsp. (to start) salt, plus pepper and allspice. Cook until meat is brown.

3 Add milk. When it begins to simmer, reduce heat to low and cook at a gentle simmer, stirring occasionally, until milk has mostly boiled away, about 30 minutes. Add white wine and cook as with milk, until it has mostly boiled away. Add tomatoes and juice; bring to a simmer. Cover pot, reduce heat to low, and allow sauce to cook very gently at barest simmer, 2½ to 3 hours. Season to taste with remaining salt.

4 Just before sauce is done, bring a pot of water to boil, salt it generously, and boil pasta according to package directions. Drain, mix with a third of sauce, then serve with remaining sauce on top with lots of grated cheese.

Makes 4 cups sauce.

194

Spaghetti Carbonara

Created by Susan Chumsky

Heavy cream complements the salty pancetta, and the grated pecorino cheese adds some welcome bite.

2 Tbsp. olive oil

6 ounces pancetta or thick bacon, cut into 1-inch-long, thin strips

1 small onion, finely chopped

1 ½ pounds spaghetti

2 Tbsp. coarse sea salt

2 large egg yolks

2 Tbsp. chopped parsley

⅓ cup grated pecorino cheese, plus more for garnish

⅓ cup heavy cream

½ tsp. coarsely ground black pepper

1 Heat olive oil in a large skillet over medium heat. Add pancetta and cook 5 minutes. Add onion and sauté until both onion and pancetta are lightly browned. Remove from heat.

2 Meanwhile, cook pasta according to package directions, in boiling water with sea salt. While pasta cooks, stir together yolks, parsley, and ⅓ cup cheese. Return pancetta and onion to medium heat; add cream and pepper and bring to a slow simmer.

3 Strain pasta, reserving 1¼ cups of pasta water. Blend ¼ cup of pasta water with yolk mixture, then stir into pancetta cream sauce. Add ½ to ¾ cup more of pasta water and simmer sauce until bubbling and slightly thickened, about 1 minute.

4 Return pasta to pot and toss with sauce. If necessary, add more pasta water to make sauce creamy. Serve with additional grated cheese on the side, if desired.

Makes 6 servings.

196

Caesar Pasta with Baby Romaine & Parmesan

Chef: Rori Trovato

Romaine lettuce, anchovies, croutons, lemon juice, garlic, and Parmesan belong together on the tongue.

1 cup seasoned croutons

2 Tbsp. sea salt

1 pound linguine

¼ cup extra-virgin olive oil

4 to 6 anchovy fillets (more or less, according to your taste), minced

1 Tbsp. capers, rinsed and dried

3 whole garlic cloves, minced

12 heads baby romaine or 3 heads regular romaine, tough bases removed, cut into fourths crosswise (about 3-inch pieces)

½ tsp. cracked black pepper

¼ cup lemon juice

½ cup freshly grated Parmesan cheese, plus additional for table

Salt and freshly ground pepper

1 In a food processor, pulse croutons into large crumbs. Set aside.

2 Bring a large saucepan filled with water to a boil. Add sea salt. Cook pasta according to package directions. Strain and reserve ½ cup pasta water.

3 Meanwhile, heat olive oil in a large sauté pan over medium-high heat. Add anchovies and capers and sauté 2 to 3 minutes. Add garlic, lettuce, cracked pepper, and lemon juice. Sauté just until lettuce wilts, about 1 minute. Stir in cooked linguine and Parmesan; if dry, add reserved pasta water. Season with salt and pepper to taste. Divide into individual pasta bowls and top with bread crumbs.

Makes 4 servings.

English Pea Risotto with Black Trumpet Mushrooms

Chef: Julia McClaskey

You won't go stir-crazy if you follow this foolproof technique for cooking risotto.

- 2 Tbsp. plus ½ tsp. salt
- 2 pounds (2 cups) fresh English peas, shelled (if not available, substitute small green peas)
- 2 Tbsp. olive oil
- ¼ tsp. black pepper
- 5 to 6 cups warm chicken stock
- 4 Tbsp. unsalted butter
- 2 small yellow onions, finely chopped
- 2 cups arborio rice
- 1 cup dry white wine
- 1 cup grated Parmesan cheese
- 3 cups fresh black trumpet mushrooms (if not available, substitute chanterelle or portobello mushrooms, but do not blanch; sauté only)
- 3 shallots, minced
- ½ bunch fresh thyme
- 3 tsp. white truffle oil

1 In a large saucepan, bring water to a boil with 2 Tbsp. salt. Cook peas in boiling water until soft, 5 to 7 minutes, then drain the peas and plunge them into ice water. Reserve 1 cup of cooked peas; set aside. Place the other cup of peas in a blender with 1 Tbsp. olive oil, ¼ tsp. salt, ⅛ tsp. pepper, and about 1 Tbsp. water; blend on high speed until mixture forms a smooth paste. Set aside.

2 To make risotto: Bring chicken stock to a boil in a large saucepan; reduce heat and simmer. In a large, deep skillet, melt 1 Tbsp. butter. Add onions and cook over medium-high heat until translucent. Add rice and stir rapidly until grains are coated with butter. Add wine and cook until almost evaporated, stirring constantly. Add ½ cup of chicken stock and cook, stirring, until almost evaporated. (Rice should never get completely dry or soupy.) Add another ½ cup of stock, cooking and stirring until almost evaporated. Continue process for 20 to 25 minutes, until rice is almost tender and mixture is creamy. Stir in 1 Tbsp. butter, English pea paste, whole peas, and grated Parmesan.

3 To cook mushrooms: Bring another saucepan of water to a boil; add black trumpet mushrooms and cook 3 seconds to remove excess dirt. Drain and cool on a cookie sheet.

4 Heat a large skillet to the point of smoking. Add 1 Tbsp. olive oil and mushrooms and sauté 1 minute. Add shallots, thyme, and remaining butter, salt, and pepper. Sauté 2 more minutes.

5 To serve: Spoon risotto into wide, shallow bowls; top with mushrooms. Drizzle each bowl with ½ tsp. truffle oil.

Makes 6 servings.

Arugula & Barley Tabbouleh

Chef: Rori Trovato

Arugula—in place of the classic parsley—and a dash of jalapeño
add bite and lemony spice to this tabbouleh.

½ cup barley

Kosher salt

2 cups arugula, loosely packed

3 scallions, roughly chopped

1 ½ tsp. minced garlic (about ½ clove)

1 cup parsley leaves, loosely packed

1 small jalapeño, seeded and minced

3 Tbsp. olive oil

¼ cup lemon juice (about 2 lemons),
    plus more to taste

½ tsp. black pepper

¾ cup (about 4 ounces) crumbled feta
    cheese

1 Place barley, ½ tsp. salt, and 2½ cups water in a medium saucepan. Bring to a boil, then reduce heat to medium-low. Simmer until grains are tender but chewy, about 30 minutes. Drain and rinse under cold water until cooled. Set aside.

2 In the bowl of a food processor, combine arugula, scallions, garlic, parsley, and jalapeño. Process until finely chopped, scraping mixture down sides of bowl as needed. Add olive oil, lemon juice, 1 tsp. salt, and pepper, and pulse until blended.

3 In a bowl, combine arugula mixture with barley and feta. Season with additional salt or lemon juice, if desired.

Makes 4 servings.

202

Mango Couscous

Chef: Marcus Samuelsson

This fruity couscous tastes great with chicken or pork—or just about anything.

1 cup couscous

2 Tbsp. olive oil

1 garlic clove, minced

1 mango, peeled, pitted, and cut into
    1-inch cubes (about 1 cup)

1 jalapeño chili, seeds and ribs
    removed, finely chopped

½ cup raisins

1 ripe tomato, chopped

Juice of 1 lime (about 2 Tbsp.)

¼ cup chopped cilantro

¼ cup chopped parsley

1 Prepare couscous according to package directions. Fluff with a fork and set aside.

2 Heat 1 Tbsp. olive oil in a large sauté pan over high heat. Add garlic, mango, and jalapeño. Sauté until mango begins to color, about 1 minute.

3 Stir in remaining 1 Tbsp. olive oil, couscous, raisins, tomato, lime juice, cilantro, and parsley, and toss to heat through, about 1 minute. Season with ½ tsp. salt and serve hot or at room temperature.

Makes 4 servings.

Brown Rice Risotto

Chef: Colin Cowie

This risotto is so easy, you'll be encouraged to experiment with all sorts
of additions, such as mushrooms, asparagus, and seafood.

2 ½ cups chicken stock
1 Tbsp. butter
1 cup long-grain brown rice
1 cup grated Parmesan cheese
Chopped parsley, for garnish

1 Bring chicken stock to a boil. Add butter. Once butter is melted, stir in the rice and reduce heat to simmer. Cover and cook 45 to 50 minutes. The rice should be moist.

2 Remove from heat and fluff with a fork. Stir in cheese, garnish with parsley, and serve immediately.

Serves 2 as a main course or 10 to 12 as a cocktail party appetizer.

Variations

■ MUSHROOMS

Prepare risotto through step 1. As rice cooks, wipe clean, trim, and slice ½ pound assorted mushrooms (cremini, white jumbo, and shiitake) into ¼-inch slices. In a large skillet, heat 2 Tbsp. butter over medium-high heat. Add mushrooms and cook uncovered 6 minutes, stirring regularly. Remove from heat. Add mushrooms and liquid to cooked rice. Mix well. Stir in Parmesan, then garnish with parsley; serve immediately.

Makes 2 servings.

■ ASPARAGUS

Prepare risotto through step 1. As rice cooks, clean and peel ½ pound medium asparagus (approximately 15 spears). Trim bottoms so that stalks measure about 5 inches (discard ends or save to use in a vegetable soup). Rinse asparagus and place in a single layer in a glass microwave-safe baking dish. Add 1½ Tbsp. water and cover with a damp paper towel. Cook on high for 2½ minutes, until cooked through but still crisp. Remove stalks and cut each into 5 equal pieces. (Optional: Toss asparagus with 1 Tbsp. truffle oil.) When rice is done, fluff and stir in cheese. Mix in asparagus, garnish with parsley, and serve immediately.

Makes 2 servings.

■ SEAFOOD

2 Tbsp. olive oil
¾ pound jumbo shrimp, peeled, deveined, tails removed, cut into thirds
3 Tbsp. chopped shallots
½ pound cooked lobster tail, removed from shell and cut into ¾-inch pieces

Prepare risotto through step 1, substituting 2½ cups water for chicken stock. When rice is cooked, remove from heat, fluff with a fork, and stir in ¾ cup grated Parmesan. Meanwhile, in a large skillet, heat 2 Tbsp. olive oil over medium-high heat. Add shrimp, scallops, and chopped shallots and sauté 2 minutes. Add lobster tail and cook an additional minute, until all items are cooked through. Remove seafood from heat and add to cooked rice. Garnish with parsley and serve immediately.

Makes 4 servings.

Cuban Grilled Corn on the Cob with Queso Blanco & Lime

Chef: Rori Trovato

This incredible grilled corn is slathered with chili powder, paprika, and lime.

4 ears corn in husks, silks removed
2 tsp. chili powder
1 tsp. paprika
1 Tbsp. salt
6 Tbsp. (¾ stick) butter
½ cup finely grated queso blanco
1 lime, cut into quarters

1 In a large saucepan filled with salted boiling water, cook corn in husks 8 minutes. Meanwhile, in a small bowl, combine chili powder, paprika, and salt.

2 On a medium grill or in a broiler, grill corn just until char marks are visible on husks. Remove and let cool. Pull back husks, rub corn with butter, and sprinkle with cheese and paprika mixture. Serve with lime wedges.

Makes 4 servings.

204

Creamy Corn Pudding with Cheddar Cheese & Chives

Chef: Rori Trovato

The pudding is creamy as all get-out yet tastes as light as a soufflé.

4 slices white bread, crusts removed
1 Tbsp. extra-virgin olive oil
1 tsp. minced garlic
6 ears corn, kernels removed
1 onion, chopped
½ cup milk
5 eggs, slightly beaten
½ cup heavy cream
1 Tbsp. salt
2 cups (8 ounces) grated Cheddar cheese
½ cup chopped chives

1 Preheat oven to 325°. In a food processor, pulse bread until large crumbs form. In baking dish, combine bread crumbs, olive oil, and garlic, then bake 7 to 12 minutes, until golden and slightly crisp. Remove and let cool.

2 Butter a 3-quart baking dish; set aside. In a large saucepan, combine corn, onion, and milk. Bring to a boil, reduce heat, and simmer 5 minutes.

3 Remove from heat. Add eggs, cream, salt, 1½ cups cheese, and chives. Stir well and pour into dish; bake 30 minutes. Add bread crumbs and remaining ½ cup cheese; continue baking 20 to 25 minutes, or until a knife inserted in middle comes out clean. Serve hot.

Makes 6 to 8 servings.

Cuban Grilled Corn on the Cob
with Queso Blanco & Lime

Beet-Ginger Chutney
(recipe on page 213)

Chapter 9

SAUCES, DRESSINGS, & CONDIMENTS

Olive Oil Vinaigrette

Chef: Alison Mesrop

With a versatile vinaigrette, you can glaze, drizzle, and splash
everything from salads to chicken to fish.

2 garlic cloves
½ cup vinegar (such as white, sherry,
   cider, port, or champagne vinegar)
1 ½ tsp. Dijon mustard
Salt and freshly ground black pepper
1 ½ cups extra-virgin olive oil
¼ cup finely chopped shallots or red
   onion

In a food processor with metal blade attached, mince garlic. Add vinegar, mustard, ¾ tsp. salt, and ¾ tsp. pepper. Process to combine. With the motor running, slowly drizzle in oil until dressing is emulsified. Taste, and add additional salt and pepper if necessary. Pour into a bowl and stir in shallots. Stir before using.

Makes 2 ¼ cups.

Variations

■ RED WINE
Use red wine vinegar in recipe above.

■ BALSAMIC
In place of the ½ cup vinegar, use ¼ cup red wine or balsamic vinegar. In place of the 1½ cups olive oil, use 1¼ cups olive oil.

■ BASIL
In place of the ½ cup vinegar, use ¾ cup balsamic vinegar and ¼ cup fresh lemon juice. Stir in ¼ to ½ cup chopped fresh basil with shallots.

■ GREEK LEMON-OREGANO
In place of the ½ cup vinegar, use ¼ cup red wine or cider vinegar and ¼ cup fresh lemon juice. Stir in ¼ cup chopped fresh oregano or 1 Tbsp. dried oregano with shallots.

■ CILANTRO-CUMIN
In place of the ½ cup vinegar, use ¼ cup cider vinegar and ¼ cup fresh lime juice. In place of the 1½ cups olive oil, use ¾ cup olive oil and ¾ cup canola oil. Stir in 1½ tsp. ground cumin and ¼ to ½ cup chopped fresh cilantro with shallots.

■ MINT-CUMIN
In place of the ½ cup vinegar, use 2½ Tbsp. red wine vinegar, 2½ Tbsp. cider vinegar, and 2½ Tbsp. fresh lemon juice. Replace black pepper with ½ tsp. ground white pepper. Stir in 1½ tsp. ground cumin and ¼ to ½ cup chopped fresh mint with shallots.

■ PORT
In a 1-quart saucepan, bring 1 cup port to a boil. Reduce the heat slightly and boil until reduced to 2 Tbsp., about 8 minutes. Let cool. In place of the ½ cup vinegar, use ¼ cup sherry vinegar, ¼ cup balsamic vinegar, and reduced port. In place of the 1½ cups olive oil, use ¾ cup olive oil and ¾ cup canola oil. Replace mustard with 1 Tbsp. tomato paste.

■ MUSTARD-DILL
In place of the ½ cup vinegar, use ¼ cup cider vinegar and ¼ cup champagne vinegar. Increase mustard to ¼ cup (you can use Dijon, whole grain, or spicy brown mustard, or any combination of the three) and add 2 Tbsp. firmly packed brown sugar. Replace olive oil with canola oil. Stir in ½ cup chopped fresh dill with shallots.

■ ROASTED GARLIC
Preheat oven to 350°. Place 8 large peeled garlic cloves on a doubled sheet of aluminum foil. Drizzle with 1 tsp. olive oil and sprinkle with ¼ tsp. salt. Wrap garlic and bake until very soft, about 45 minutes; let cool. After mincing fresh garlic, add roasted garlic and finely chop. In place of the ½ cup vinegar, use ¼ cup red wine vinegar and ¼ cup balsamic vinegar.

Ginger-Carrot Dressing

Chef: Alison Mesrop

½ pound (about 4 medium-size) carrots, peeled and sliced

1 garlic clove

One (1-inch) piece fresh ginger, peeled

⅓ cup fresh orange juice

¼ cup tomato juice

2 to 3 Tbsp. cider vinegar, or fresh lime or lemon juice

½ tsp. salt

In a small saucepan, cover carrots with water. Bring to a boil. Reduce heat and simmer, covered, until tender, about 14 minutes. Drain and let cool. In a food processor with metal blade attached, mince garlic and ginger. Add cooked carrots and process until carrots are quite smooth, occasionally pausing processor to scrape sides of bowl. Add orange and tomato juices, vinegar, and salt. Process until smooth, drizzling in water as needed if dressing is too thick. Pour into a bowl, cover, and refrigerate until serving, up to 1 week. Stir before using.

Makes 1⅓ cups.

Buttermilk Ranch Dressing

Chef: Alison Mesrop

1½ cups buttermilk or plain whole-milk yogurt

1 cup mayonnaise

1 to 2 Tbsp. cider vinegar

1 Tbsp. dehydrated onion flakes

½ tsp. salt

½ tsp. freshly ground black pepper

In a medium bowl, whisk together all ingredients until smooth. Cover and refrigerate at least 30 minutes or up to 1 week before serving. Stir before using.

Makes about 2½ cups.

Roquefort Dressing

Chef: Alison Mesrop

1 cup plain whole-milk yogurt

½ cup mayonnaise

2 Tbsp. fresh lemon juice

1 garlic clove, minced

¼ tsp. salt

¼ tsp. freshly ground black pepper

½ to ¾ cup crumbled Roquefort cheese

1 Tbsp. chopped fresh tarragon (optional)

In a medium bowl, whisk together all ingredients. Cover and refrigerate until serving, up to 1 week. Stir before using.

Makes about 2 cups.

Tomato & Onion Raita

Chef: Colin Cowie

This tangy topping is a perfect accompaniment for all kinds of soups.

⅓ cup red wine or cider vinegar
2 Tbsp. olive oil
1 Tbsp. sugar
½ tsp. salt
¼ tsp. freshly ground black pepper
3 large ripe tomatoes (about 2 pounds), stemmed, seeded, and diced
½ medium white onion, finely chopped
2 Tbsp. chopped fresh cilantro
1 small jalapeño chili, stemmed, seeded, and chopped

In a medium bowl, whisk vinegar, oil, 2 Tbsp. water, sugar, salt, and pepper until blended. Add remaining ingredients and toss until well combined. Cover and refrigerate at least 2 hours, or up to 24 hours, before serving. Serve chilled.

Makes 3 cups.

Banana–Papaya Salsa

Chef: Alison Mesrop

Bananas make this salsa so much more than a dip.

2 cups chopped papaya
1 medium red onion, finely chopped
½ cup chopped cilantro (about ½ bunch)
¼ cup fresh lime juice
¼ cup cider vinegar
1 jalapeño chili, seeded and minced
2 tsp. kosher salt, or to taste
1 tsp. freshly ground pepper, or to taste
2 cups chopped banana (firm and slightly underripe)

In a bowl, combine all ingredients except banana. Cover and refrigerate until ready to serve; add banana just before serving.

Makes 4 cups.

This salsa can be made up to four hours in advance.

Fresh Cranberry Relish

Chef: Govind Armstrong

Fresh cranberries with a twist!

Two (12-ounce) bags fresh cranberries
1 cup sugar
¼ cup orange liqueur (such as Grand Marnier)
Zest and juice from 1 navel orange

Place all ingredients in a food processor; pulse several times until mixture is chunky.

Makes 4 ½ cups.

Mango Chutney

Chef: Colin Cowie

Serve this fruit-filled chutney with grilled meats, atop goat cheese, or alongside hard, aged cheeses.

6 large, firm ripe mangoes (about 6 pounds), peeled, pitted, and cut crosswise into thin slices
1 cup cider vinegar
1 cup firmly packed light brown sugar
10 garlic cloves, peeled and thinly sliced
One (1-inch) piece fresh ginger, peeled and thinly sliced
1 tsp. ground red (cayenne) pepper
½ tsp. salt

1 Place ingredients in a 4-quart heavy saucepan over medium-high heat and simmer 1 hour, uncovered, stirring occasionally to prevent sticking, until chutney thickens.

2 Remove from heat and transfer to a bowl; allow to cool, store in an airtight jar, and refrigerate until ready to serve.

Makes about 5 ¼ cups.

At the Table with Rori Trovato
COMMON SENSE TEMPERED BY ENTHUSIASM

"When I create a recipe, I look at the primary ingredient and try to think outside the box," says cookbook author, food stylist, teacher, and caterer Rori Trovato. "But I also think about how I would like to eat that particular food. I put the two together and decide how I might get someone else to try it."

Over the years, Rori has developed a lion's share of the recipes for *O, The Oprah Magazine* and says that every time she writes a recipe for a home cook, she hopes she is "making an itty bitty contribution" to getting people back into the kitchen.

"When I teach, students often tell me they know nothing," she continues. "With a little prodding, I discover there's always something they know. They might recall a dish their mother or grandmother cooked, or something they tried when they were first married."

She is endlessly fascinated by what she calls the genealogy of cooking. How we cook is based on what we've been taught as children, Rori says, whether we realize it or not, and cooking styles can be traced through a family's generations.

For example, Rori says, Thanksgiving is our one true culinary tradition in America, and she would hate to see it change. But except for a turkey-with-all-the-trimmings feast, she is all for experimentation in the kitchen.

"Listen to your instincts," she suggests. "Do not ignore what you like. If you don't like something, you probably won't be good at it."

She tries to make the recipes she writes accessible to home cooks, and she urges you to follow any recipe closely until you feel proficient. When you do, she says, go with your heart and taste buds to cook food as you like it. Most of all, she hopes her readers will want to cook.

"I want people to realize that braising only takes about 15 minutes of your time; the rest of the time the food is in the oven. Because a homemade cake is so much better than one from a mix, someone might be willing to make the extra effort to bake one," she says.

"The little things make a big difference, like chopping your own garlic, squeezing juice from a real lemon, mixing a little orange juice and melted butter into maple syrup for pancakes, and making real hot chocolate, which is so easy and so special."

> "Do not ignore what you like. If you don't like something, you probably won't be good at it."

Rori, the author of *Dishing with Style,* believes it's important to set a pleasing table. When she makes a meal, she aims to fill the plates with color and texture as well as flavor. She wants the food to be memorable and explosively exciting, she says, and yet she prefers to keep it simple. "I really don't like overmanipulated food," she says.

Her recipes are designed to expand home cooks' abilities without "scaring them." Her advice is always practical (don't try something new for a dinner party; give it a trial run first), but her expectations and enthusiasm are inspiring.

"Once you learn a few things, your whole experience in the kitchen will be more rewarding," she promises.

Rori Trovato's Recipes

Beet-Ginger Chutney

Chef: Marcus Samuelsson

The sweetness of the ginger and cardamom play well with the earthiness of the beets. Try this with any poultry dish.

2 Tbsp. olive oil

4 shallots, finely chopped

4 garlic cloves, minced

Two (3-inch) pieces ginger, peeled and sliced

4 beets (about 2 pounds), peeled and cut into ½-inch cubes

2 Tbsp. honey

4 white or green cardamom pods*

2 thyme sprigs

2 Tbsp. sugar

1 Tbsp. unsalted butter

2 cups chicken stock or broth

Salt to taste

*You can find cardamom pods at savoryspiceshop.com.

1 Heat oil in a large, deep sauté pan over high heat. Add shallots, garlic, ginger, and beets; reduce heat to low and sauté 10 minutes, stirring occasionally.

2 Add honey, cardamom, thyme, sugar, and butter; stir 1 minute. Add chicken stock and bring to a simmer; cook until beets are tender and most of stock has evaporated, 45 to 50 minutes.

3 Remove from heat. Discard thyme, ginger, and cardamom; stir in ¼ tsp. salt, or to taste. Let cool before serving.

Makes 3 cups.

Delicious with roast turkey breast, this chutney keeps for up to two weeks if refrigerated in an airtight container.

213

Pumpkin Applesauce Muffins
(recipe on page 230)

Chapter 10

BISCUITS, BREADS, & MUFFINS

Oprah's Corn Fritters

Created by Oprah Winfrey and Art Smith

These Southern-style fritters are just right with maple syrup, fruit syrup, or honey.

2 ears corn, shucked, or ½ cup frozen
    or canned corn
⅔ cup yellow cornmeal*
⅓ cup self-rising flour*
1 cup buttermilk
1 egg, beaten
2 Tbsp. melted unsalted butter,
    optional
Milk or water, if needed

*White Lily cornmeal and flour, which
make perfect fritters, are available at
www.whitelily.com.

1 Microwave the corn on high for 2 or 3 minutes. Slice off the kernels, and set them aside.

2 In a bowl, mix the cornmeal and the flour well, using a wire whisk. This will make your fritters very light. In a separate bowl, whisk together the buttermilk and the egg. Gradually add the wet ingredients to the dry—Oprah likes using a fork. Don't worry if the batter isn't completely combined; you want to be careful not to overmix it. Fold in the corn and add the butter if desired. If the result is thicker than pancake batter, thin it with a little milk or water.

3 Heat a skillet or a griddle to medium, spray with Pam, and add spoonfuls of batter. Cook the fritters for 2 minutes per side. A great way to tell if they're ready to turn is to look for little bubbles all over the surface. You might have to make a few fritters before they start coming out perfectly. Serve with honey or your favorite syrup.

Makes 4 servings.

The Harlem Tea Room's Scones

Chef: Patrice Clayton

Hot, crumbly, buttery scones are heaven with a cup of freshly brewed tea.
Try them baked with cheese and thyme, or perhaps with plump raisins.

8 Tbsp. (1 stick) cold, unsalted butter, cut into small pieces, plus extra for baking sheets
3 ½ cups all-purpose flour
2 tsp. baking soda
2 tsp. cream of tartar
½ tsp. salt
1 ½ cups sour cream or buttermilk
1 egg, beaten, or milk, for brushing scones

1 Preheat oven to 450°. Coat two baking sheets with butter. Sift flour, baking soda, cream of tartar, and salt into a large bowl. Add 8 Tbsp. butter, using fingertips to combine until mixture takes on texture of fine meal. Add sour cream and stir until flour mixture is just moist and dough begins to stick together. Gather dough into a ball and knead lightly until fully integrated.

2 Place dough on a floured work surface and roll with a floured rolling pin to ¾ inch thick. Dip a 2-inch cutter into flour and cut out scones as close to one another as possible. Place on prepared baking sheets, with space in between; let stand 10 minutes. Brush tops with egg, and bake until golden brown, 10 to 12 minutes. Remove to wire rack to cool. Serve warm with butter, clotted cream, whipped cream, fruit preserves, or jam.

Makes about 1 ½ dozen.

Variations

■ BAKING POWDER SCONES

Omit baking soda and cream of tartar and substitute 4 tsp. baking powder in dry ingredients. Replace sour cream with 1 ¼ cups milk.

■ CHEDDAR-THYME SCONES

After combining butter and dry ingredients, stir 1 ½ cups grated Cheddar cheese and 1 Tbsp. chopped fresh thyme into flour mixture before adding sour cream. Sprinkle tops of scones with an additional ½ cup grated Cheddar cheese before baking.

■ RAISIN SCONES

Add ¼ cup sugar to dry ingredients. After combining butter and flour mixture, stir in 1 cup raisins.

217

Focaccia with Caramelized Onions, Goat Cheese, & Rosemary

Chef: Art Smith

Focaccia is the perfect canvas for culinary experimentation—it's a thrillingly versatile Italian flatbread that rises to every occasion.

DOUGH

1 cup warm water (105° to 115°)

One (¼-ounce) package active dry yeast

½ tsp. honey

¼ cup extra-virgin olive oil, plus more for greasing

1 tsp. sea salt

3 cups bread flour, plus more for dusting

TOPPING

2 Tbsp. (¼ stick) unsalted butter

3 medium yellow onions, halved and cut into ¼-inch-thick slices

½ tsp. sea salt

¼ tsp. freshly ground pepper

½ cup crumbled goat cheese

2 Tbsp. coarsely chopped fresh rosemary (or 1 Tbsp. dried)

Extra-virgin olive oil, for drizzling

1 To make dough: In a large bowl with a wooden spoon or in the bowl of a heavy-duty mixer, combine water, yeast, and honey; stir to dissolve. Let stand until foamy, about 5 minutes.

2 Add oil and salt to yeast mixture. With spoon or with mixer on low speed, gradually add 2½ cups flour until a soft dough forms. Slowly add remaining flour until dough just begins to pull away from sides of bowl. Remove dough from bowl and knead by hand on a lightly floured surface until smooth and elastic, about 8 minutes; add more flour as needed to keep dough from sticking. Or keep dough in bowl, change to a dough hook, and increase speed to medium; knead until smooth and supple, about 5 minutes.

3 Form dough into a ball and place in a large, lightly greased bowl; turn to coat. Cover bowl tightly with plastic wrap and let dough rise in a warm place until doubled in volume, about 1 hour.

4 To make topping: In a large skillet, melt butter over medium heat. Add onions, ¼ teaspoon salt, and ⅛ teaspoon pepper and cook, stirring frequently, until onions are golden brown, about 20 minutes. Cool.

5 Preheat oven to 425°. Lightly grease an 11" x 17" jelly-roll pan; punch down dough and pat it into pan. (If dough pulls back from edges, cover loosely with greased plastic wrap, let stand for 5 minutes, then pat out again.) Cover loosely with greased plastic wrap and let rise in a warm place until almost doubled, about 30 minutes.

6 Using fingertips, dimple surface of dough. Arrange onions over top, then sprinkle with goat cheese, rosemary, and remaining ¼ tsp. salt and ⅛ tsp. pepper. Lightly drizzle with olive oil. Bake in lower third of oven until golden brown, about 25 minutes. Cool before serving.

Makes 12 servings (6 sandwiches).

Cheesy Garlic Bread

Chef: Rori Trovato

Who doesn't love garlic bread? This is one of our favorites.

- ¼ cup extra-virgin olive oil
- 1 head garlic
- 5 Tbsp. unsalted butter, softened
- ¾ cup grated Parmesan cheese
- 2 Tbsp. grated Pecorino Romano cheese
- 1 Tbsp. chopped thyme leaves
- 1 tsp. salt
- ¼ tsp. freshly ground pepper
- ½ tsp. paprika
- ¼ tsp. red pepper flakes (optional)
- 1 loaf store-bought or homemade rustic country bread, cut into ½-inch slices

1 Preheat oven to 400°. Using about 1 tsp. olive oil, brush garlic head. Wrap garlic in foil and roast until very tender, about 50 minutes. Remove from oven, and when cool enough to handle, cut off top and squeeze roasted garlic from skin into a medium bowl.

2 Add remaining ingredients except bread. Mix well. Spread mixture onto each slice of bread, reserving about ¼ cup. Wrap bread in foil, with foil seam on top. Bake about 20 minutes. Carefully open seam of foil completely. Brush bread with remaining ¼ cup garlic mixture and continue cooking on foil until golden brown and crispy, about 12 minutes. Serve hot.

Makes about 12 slices.

Rosemary-Parmesan Biscuits

Chef: Gail Monaghan

These small cheese biscuits are almost addictive.

- 1 cup all-purpose flour
- ½ cup chopped walnuts, toasted
- 1 Tbsp. finely chopped fresh rosemary
- ½ tsp. salt
- Pinch of cayenne pepper
- Pinch of freshly ground black pepper
- 1 stick butter
- 1 ½ cups freshly grated Parmesan cheese (6 ounces)

1 In a large bowl, stir together the flour, walnuts, rosemary, salt, and peppers.

2 With a mixer on medium-high speed, cream butter in a medium bowl until light and fluffy, about 3 minutes. Add cheese and beat on low speed until well combined. Add the flour mixture and beat just until blended.

3 Divide the dough into 2 pieces and roll each piece into a 1½-inch-diameter log. Wrap each log in plastic wrap and refrigerate at least 30 minutes, or until easy to slice.

4 Preheat the oven to 350°. Grease 2 large baking sheets.

5 Cut the logs crosswise into ⅜-inch-thick slices and place flat on baking sheets. Bake 12 to 15 minutes, or until golden brown. Transfer to wire racks to cool.

Makes about 36 biscuits.

Cheesy Garlic Bread

Banana-Pecan Honey Bread

Created by Susan Chumsky

Milk and honey transform this banana bread into an extraordinary and distinctive loaf.

2 ½ cups plus 1 Tbsp. all-purpose flour
2 tsp. baking powder
1 tsp. salt
¾ tsp. baking soda
3 ripe bananas, mashed (1½ cups)
¼ cup whole milk
½ cup honey
1 Tbsp. vanilla extract
1 stick butter, softened
½ cup sugar
2 eggs
1 cup pecans, toasted

1 Preheat oven to 350°. Grease a 9" x 5" loaf pan and line the bottom with parchment or waxed paper. Sift together 2½ cups flour, baking powder, salt, and baking soda; set aside. In a small bowl, combine bananas, milk, honey, and vanilla. Set aside.

2 In the bowl of a mixer, beat butter and sugar at medium speed until fluffy. Beat in eggs, one at a time. Reduce speed to low and alternately add flour mixture and banana mixture, beginning and ending with flour. Beat just until blended. In a small bowl, combine nuts with remaining 1 Tbsp. flour and mix well; add to batter. Pour into prepared pan. Bake until a toothpick inserted in center of bread comes out clean, about 1 hour 10 minutes. Cool on a wire rack 10 minutes.

3 Run a knife around inside rim of pan to remove bread, peel off paper from bottom, and cool completely on a wire rack.

Makes 8 servings (16 slices).

222

Gayle King recalls a meeting she attended not too long ago where, in the course of his presentation, a co-worker mentioned a restaurant that served "truffle oil French fries." From that moment, he had Gayle's rapt attention. Although the meeting had nothing to do with food, she raised her hand with a question.

"Is there really a restaurant that makes truffle oil French fries?" she asked with wonder and awe.

Gayle, who is the editor-at-large of *O, The Oprah Magazine* and the host of *The Gayle King Show* on XM Radio, is a food lover. Not a cook, as she is quick to point out. She can make pancakes and scrambled eggs with cheese and crispy bacon on the side, but that about sums up her abilities in the kitchen. "My two kids won't have fond food memories from their childhoods," she says. They will remember, however, that their mother absolutely, unequivocally adores food and eating.

When she took her son to college recently, she noticed an entry on the hotel's room service menu for peach bread pudding. Yum! She was instantly tantalized. Later in the evening, while buying dorm room supplies at Target, she realized she would not get back to the hotel before the kitchen closed. She placed a hurried phone call to the front desk with a request. Could the pudding be waiting in her room for her? It was, and it was sublime.

Gayle may not cook but she is a fan of tasteful presentation and pleasing surroundings when she eats. She loves fine dining in elegant restaurants as much as she appreciates a juicy cheeseburger in the right joint. When she talks to a friend who has attended a gala she missed, her first questions are not about the guest list or the fashion but the menu. She admits that when she's a guest at a large buffet party, it's hard for her not to be the first in line for the food.

> "I have an impressionable palate. A well-worded menu or beautifully presented dish excites me. I get a great deal of pleasure just thinking about food."

"I have an impressionable palate," she explains. "A well-worded menu or beautifully presented dish excites me. I get a great deal of pleasure just thinking about food."

She fantasizes about owning a restaurant where everyone is greeted joyfully at the door, seated immediately, and offered a basket of hot, freshly baked rolls with sweet, creamy butter. "Really good bread is intoxicating," she says.

As a magazine editor, Gayle is certainly aware of the health benefits of eating fruits, vegetables, and whole grains, but that doesn't stop her from ordering French fries. Oprah laughs at her good friend when she grills a waiter about the kind a restaurant serves. "There's a science to ordering potatoes," Gayle says. "Are they skinny shoestring or big, fat steak fries? You just have to let your tastebuds guide you when deciding what to eat." As for dessert, Gayle has a sweet tooth. "I'll do almost anything for cake—even trample little children!" she says jokingly.

In fact, leaving Los Angeles one afternoon for the ride to the airport, she asked the driver to stop at Sprinkles Cupcakes in Beverly Hills, a bakery that makes one of her favorite treats. "When we pulled up, there was a long line out the door," she remembers. "I called American Airlines to ask if it would be possible for them to meet me at the curb and help me to the gate. Even with their help I knew I'd be taking a chance and could miss the plane, and so I made the executive decision to fly to New York cupcake-free." It was a sacrifice she still regrets today.

Whether she's describing the cupcakes that got away or a long-ago fabulous meal that she's still passionate about, Gayle's enthusiasm for good food is compelling: One goes away from the conversation with an appetite for more.

Candied Orange-Apricot Bread

Created by Susan Quick

This recipe involves a little more work than most tea breads, but it's one of the best ever.

3 medium oranges
¾ cup plus ¼ cup granulated sugar
1 ½ cups chopped dried apricots
3 Tbsp. minced crystallized ginger
2 ½ cups all-purpose flour
2 tsp. baking powder
¼ tsp. salt
½ cup milk
1 Tbsp. orange liqueur, such as Cointreau, Grand Marnier, or Triple Sec (optional)
1 stick unsalted butter, room temperature
2 large eggs
Confectioners' sugar, for dusting

1 Using a vegetable peeler, remove bright orange outer zest from oranges. Thinly slice zest into slivers (you should have about ½ cup zest). Combine zest and ½ cup water in small saucepan and bring to a boil. Lower heat, cover, and simmer 5 minutes. Add ¾ cup granulated sugar and stir to dissolve. Add apricots and ginger and continue simmering, stirring occasionally, 8 to 10 minutes longer (the fruit will be candied and sticky, with almost no liquid left). Remove from heat and cool to room temperature.

2 Preheat oven to 325°. Butter a 9" x 5" x 3" loaf pan.

3 Sift together flour, baking powder, and salt.

4 Combine milk with liqueur, if desired; set aside.

5 Beat butter and remaining ¼ cup granulated sugar with an electric mixer until light and fluffy. Add eggs one at a time, beating well after each addition. Beat in the cooled orange-apricot mixture. Add flour mixture alternately with milk, beginning and ending with dry ingredients. Stir after each addition until just combined, and then scrape batter into prepared pan.

6 Bake 1 hour, or until a knife or wooden skewer inserted in the center comes out clean. Cool on a rack 10 minutes. Remove from pan and return to rack to cool completely. Wrap tightly with plastic until ready to serve. Dust with confectioners' sugar before slicing.

Makes one 9" x 5" x 3" loaf.

Simmering the orange zest, apricots, and crystallized ginger before adding them to the batter creates a pungent, brightly flavored tea bread that's even more flavorful if made a day ahead.

225

Sticky Buns

Chef: Larry Smith

Every delightful roll is an act of love.

DOUGH

One (¼-ounce) package active dry yeast
¼ cup granulated sugar
¼ cup warm water (105° to 115°)
¾ cup whole milk
2 Tbsp. (¼ stick) butter
1 large egg
3 ¾ to 4 cups all-purpose flour
½ tsp. salt

FILLING

1½ sticks butter, softened
1 ½ cups packed brown sugar
1 Tbsp. ground cinnamon
¾ cup chopped pecans or walnuts
   (optional)

FROSTING

4 ounces cream cheese, softened
1 ½ cups confectioners' sugar
1 tsp. vanilla extract

1 To make the dough: Sprinkle the yeast and a pinch of the sugar over the warm water in a large mixing bowl; let stand until foamy on top, 5 to 7 minutes. In a small bowl, microwave the milk and butter until warm, 40 to 50 seconds (105° to 115°). Add the milk and butter mixture, the remaining sugar, and the egg to the mixing bowl. Add the flour, about 1 cup at a time (adding the last ¼ cup flour if necessary), and salt, and mix (5 minutes if using a dough hook, 10 minutes if kneading by hand) until firm but soft. The dough should gently spring back when poked. Do not overknead. Place the dough in a buttered bowl; cover with plastic wrap and let rise 1 to 1½ hours, until dough has doubled in size.

2 To make the filling and assemble the buns: In a large bowl, beat the butter, brown sugar, cinnamon, and nuts (if using) until fluffy. On a lightly floured surface, press or roll the dough into a rectangle, about 17" x 14". Spread the filling evenly to all edges, leaving a ½-inch border along one of the long edges of the dough. Roll up the filling-covered dough, starting with the side opposite the edge with the border. When almost finished rolling, slightly dampen the uncovered edge with water and crimp firmly

to seal. (Roll will stretch to 22" x 3".) Using a serrated knife, cut crosswise into 12 thick slices.

3 Preheat the oven to 325°. Line a large jelly-roll pan with parchment paper. Transfer the buns to the pan, spacing evenly. Cover lightly with a towel and let stand 30 to 45 minutes, until buns are slightly puffed (not doubled). Bake 25 minutes, or until golden.

4 To make the frosting: In a medium bowl, beat the cream cheese, sugar, and vanilla until smooth. Remove buns from the oven and allow to cool just 5 minutes, then frost.

Makes 12 servings.

Jalapeño Cornbread

Chef: Norma Jean Darden

Hot and freshly baked, this bread makes almost any meal special.

4 Tbsp. (½ stick) butter, melted, plus
   1 tsp. to grease the pan
1 cup all-purpose flour
1 ½ Tbsp. sugar
2 ½ tsp. baking powder
½ tsp. salt
1 cup yellow cornmeal
2 eggs, beaten
1 ½ cups buttermilk
1 Tbsp. finely chopped pickled jalapeño
   chili

1 Preheat oven to 425°. Grease a 9-inch-square baking pan with butter.

2 In a large bowl, stir together dry ingredients with a wire whisk or fork.

3 In a medium bowl, whisk together eggs, buttermilk, melted butter, and jalapeño chili.

4 Add to cornmeal mixture and stir until just blended.

5 Pour into pan and bake 20 minutes, or until edges are golden and a toothpick inserted into the center comes out clean.

Makes 6 servings.

Jalapeño Cornbread and
Red Pepper & Fennel Soup
(soup recipe on page 57)

Pumpkin Applesauce Muffins

Chef: Nina Simonds

The two key ingredients together guarantee particularly moist, tempting muffins.

1½ Tbsp. butter, melted, or cooking spray

3 ⅓ cups all-purpose flour

2 tsp. baking soda

½ tsp. baking powder

2 tsp. ground cinnamon

½ tsp. ground cloves

½ tsp. freshly grated nutmeg

1 tsp. salt

1 stick unsalted butter, softened

2 cups sugar

4 large eggs

1 cup applesauce

1 cup canned mashed pumpkin

1 tsp. vanilla extract

⅔ cup apple juice, cider, or orange juice

1 ½ cups raisins

1 Preheat oven to 375°. Grease 12 half-cup muffin cups with melted butter. In a medium bowl, combine flour, baking soda, baking powder, cinnamon, cloves, nutmeg, and salt; set aside.

2 In a large mixing bowl, beat butter and sugar until creamy, 2 to 3 minutes. Beat in eggs, applesauce, pumpkin, and vanilla until blended. Add dry ingredients, alternating with the juice, beginning and ending with the dry mixture; mix until smooth. Fold in raisins.

3 Spoon batter into prepared muffin cups, filling each cup two-thirds full. Bake on center oven rack until a toothpick inserted in the center of each muffin comes out clean, 20 to 25 minutes. Remove from oven and allow muffins to cool in the pans several minutes; turn muffins out onto a rack. Serve warm or at room temperature. Repeat steps 1 through 3 with remaining batter.

Makes 12 muffins.

230

Sour Cream Maple-Walnut Muffins

Chef: Tom Bivins

A little fancier than some muffins, these are just right
for a weekend breakfast or brunch party.

1 ½ cups all-purpose flour
1 ½ tsp. baking powder
¼ tsp. baking soda
¼ tsp. salt
5 Tbsp. unsalted butter, softened
¼ cup plus 1 tsp. granulated sugar
¼ cup firmly packed light brown sugar
1 large egg
6 Tbsp. sour cream
6 Tbsp. Vermont maple syrup
2 Tbsp. finely chopped walnuts
⅛ tsp. ground cinnamon

1 Preheat oven to 400°. Place paper liners in 12 muffin cups.

2 In a medium bowl, stir together flour, baking powder, baking soda, and salt.

3 Using an electric mixer, cream butter, ¼ cup granulated sugar, and brown sugar on medium-high speed for 3 minutes, until light and fluffy. Add egg and beat well.

4 In a small bowl, whisk together sour cream and maple syrup.

5 On low speed, add half the dry ingredients to butter-sugar mixture. Pour in half the sour cream mixture. Add remaining dry ingredients in 2 batches, alternating with sour cream mixture. Beat until just blended.

6 In a small bowl, stir together walnuts, cinnamon, and remaining 1 tsp. granulated sugar.

7 Pour batter into muffin cups. Sprinkle top of each muffin with walnut mixture.

8 Bake until muffins are golden brown, about 20 minutes. Place tins on wire rack to cool, about 5 minutes. Remove from tins and serve warm.

Makes 12 muffins.

Banoffee Tart
(recipe on page 254)

Chapter 11

DESSERTS

12-Layer Chocolate Cake

Chef: Art Smith

Thin layers of buttery white cake sandwiched between ribbons of fudge: It's love at first bite.

CAKE

Butter, flour, and waxed paper, for coating the pans

3 sticks unsalted butter, softened

2 ¼ cups sugar

6 eggs

4 ½ cups all-purpose flour, sifted 3 times

1 ½ tsp. baking powder

Pinch of salt

3 cups milk

1 ½ tsp. vanilla extract

ICING

3 cups sugar

½ cup high-quality cocoa powder

2 sticks unsalted butter, cut into cubes

One (12-ounce) can evaporated milk

1 Tbsp. vanilla extract

Pecan halves, for garnish (optional)

1 Preheat the oven to 375°. Butter four 9-inch cake pans and line the bottoms with waxed paper, then butter the paper. Flour the pans.

2 Using a mixer, cream the softened butter and sugar. When the mixture is light and fluffy, add the eggs one at a time. Scrape the sides of the bowl with a spatula to make sure the mixture is well blended.

3 Sift together the flour, baking powder, and salt in a medium bowl. To the butter and egg mixture, gradually add the flour mixture and milk, alternating between them. Continue to scrape down the sides of the bowl. Once the flour and milk are incorporated, add the vanilla extract.

4 Add 1 cup of batter to each prepared pan and bake 10 to 12 minutes, or until light brown. Remove the layers from the pans and cool on a wire rack, placing the paper side down. Wash the pans. Butter and flour the pans again for the next batch of cakes. Repeat the process until 12 layers are baked.

5 When all the layers have cooled, make the icing. Combine the sugar, cocoa, butter, and evaporated milk in a large saucepan. Bring to a rolling boil, then reduce heat and cool 2 minutes until the icing is thin but spreadable. (This icing becomes thicker as it cools.) Add the vanilla extract.

6 Remove the waxed paper from each layer. Place one layer of cake on a wire rack and spread with icing. (For easier cleanup, assemble the cake over an edged sheet pan to collect runoff icing.) Add the next layer and ice it. Continue adding and icing layers, then pour remaining icing over the top. Icing that drips down can be used to cover the sides. Garnish with pecan halves, if desired.

Makes 20 servings.

234

Pear Upside-Down Cake

Chef: Rori Trovato

Pears are an unusual and tender twist on the usual pineapple dish.

½ cup light brown sugar

1 ½ tsp. ground cinnamon

14 Tbsp. (1 ¾ sticks) butter, softened

3 firm pears (about 1 ½ pounds), cored
and cut into ¼-inch wedges

2 cups cake flour (not self-rising)

2 tsp. baking powder

1 tsp. salt

1 tsp. ground ginger

1 ⅓ cups granulated sugar

2 eggs

2 tsp. vanilla extract

⅔ cup whole milk

2 Tbsp. fresh or dried cranberries

1 Preheat the oven to 325°. Cut a piece of parchment paper to fit the bottom of a 10-inch ovenproof skillet; set aside. In a skillet over medium-high heat, stir the brown sugar, ½ tsp. cinnamon, and 2 Tbsp. butter until melted. Add the pears. Sauté them until fork-tender and starting to brown, 5 to 7 minutes. Pour the pears and the juices into a large bowl and allow to cool slightly. Clean the skillet.

2 In a small bowl, combine the flour, baking powder, salt, remaining 1 tsp. cinnamon, and ginger. In a large bowl, with a mixer set on high speed, beat the remaining 12 Tbsp. butter and the granulated sugar until fluffy. Reduce the speed to low; beat in the eggs and vanilla until well blended. Add the flour mixture alternately with the milk, beginning and ending with the flour. Beat just until blended.

3 Coat the skillet with vegetable oil spray or butter. Place the parchment paper in the skillet and arrange the pears in overlapping circles. Pour the remaining pear juice mixture over the pears and scatter the cranberries. Carefully spoon the batter over the fruit. Using a rubber spatula, spread the mixture evenly. Bake the cake until golden brown and a toothpick

inserted in the center comes out clean, 45 to 55 minutes. Remove the cake from the oven and allow to cool for 10 minutes. Run a knife around the edges to loosen from the sides of the skillet. Invert the cake onto a serving plate. Remove the parchment paper. Serve the cake by itself or with ice cream, whipped cream, or crème fraîche.

Makes 8 servings.

Variations

■ APPLES AND CINNAMON

Substitute 3 peeled apples for the pears. When sautéing the apples in the skillet, add 1 additional tsp. ground cinnamon.

■ PUMPKIN AND MAPLE SYRUP

Peel and seed a small pumpkin and cut into ¼-inch-thick slices 3 to 4 inches long. Substitute maple syrup for the brown sugar and sauté the pumpkin meat and a quarter of the seeds 6 to 8 minutes, until fork-tender.

Coconut Lane Cake

Chef: Edna Lewis

The subtle, nutty sweetness of grated coconut made
this the legendary chef's favorite cake.

CAKE

2 sticks butter, room temperature, plus
   extra for pans
3 ½ cups cake flour, plus extra for pans
1 Tbsp. baking powder
¼ tsp. salt
1 cup milk, room temperature
1 tsp. vanilla extract
2 cups sugar
8 large egg whites, room temperature

FROSTING

12 large egg yolks
1 ½ cups sugar
1 ½ sticks unsalted butter, melted
1 ½ cups finely chopped pecans
1 ½ cups finely chopped raisins
1 ½ cups unsweetened coconut flakes
1 ½ tsp. vanilla extract
½ cup bourbon

1 To make cake: Preheat oven to
325°. Butter and flour three 9-inch cake pans; line bottoms with
parchment paper. In a small bowl,
sift together flour, baking powder,
and salt; set aside. In another small
bowl, mix together milk and
vanilla; set aside.

2 In the bowl of an electric
mixer on medium speed,
cream butter and sugar until light
and fluffy. Reduce speed and add
the flour and milk mixtures in 2 or
3 batches, beginning and ending
with flour.

3 In a separate bowl, beat egg
whites until soft peaks form.
Stir half of egg whites into batter.
Fold in remaining egg whites until
just incorporated. Pour batter into
the prepared pans and bake until
cakes are springy and edges slightly
pull away from sides of pans, 20 to
25 minutes. Remove from oven
and let cool on wire racks 10 minutes. Loosen sides with a knife and
invert cakes onto racks; remove
parchment paper and cool completely before frosting.

4 To make frosting: In a medium
saucepan over medium heat,
whisk egg yolks and sugar together
until sugar dissolves. Add melted
butter, stirring constantly until
thick enough to coat the back of a
spoon, 1 to 3 minutes; do not let
mixture simmer or boil. Add
pecans, raisins, and coconut; cook
1 minute. Remove from heat and
add vanilla and bourbon; cool to
room temperature before using.
Spread ¾ cup frosting between
each layer of cake; use the rest for
the sides and top.

Makes 8 to 10 servings.

238

Lemon Curd Cheesecake

Chef: Susan Spungen

Grand enough for a formal occasion, yet equally
appropriate for a relaxed afternoon tea.

LEMON CURD

½ cup lemon juice

6 egg yolks

1 cup sugar

4 tsp. freshly grated lemon zest

1 stick cold unsalted butter,
  cut into pieces

CRUST

1 ¼ cups graham cracker crumbs

3 Tbsp. sugar

⅛ tsp. salt

5 Tbsp. unsalted butter, melted

FILLING

2 ½ (8-ounce) packages cream cheese

½ cup plus 2 Tbsp. sugar

3 Tbsp. all-purpose flour

Salt

1 tsp. pure vanilla extract

1 tsp. freshly squeezed lemon juice

1 tsp. freshly grated lemon zest

2 large eggs, plus 1 yolk

½ cup sour cream

Melted butter, for pan

1 cup chilled lemon curd

1 To make lemon curd: Whisk together lemon juice, egg yolks, and sugar in a heavy, nonreactive 1-quart saucepan. Cook over medium-low heat, stirring constantly with a heatproof spatula or wooden spoon until mixture thickens and coats back of spoon, 5 to 10 minutes. (It should read 140° on a candy or instant-read thermometer.)

2 Remove saucepan from heat and strain mixture over a bowl. Stir in lemon zest and butter until butter completely melts. Cool slightly before using. Curd can be stored in refrigerator in an airtight container up to 1 week. Warm over a double boiler or microwave briefly to return it to liquid form. It will set up again when chilled.

3 To make crust: Preheat oven to 350°, and position rack in middle of oven. Prepare a 9-inch springform pan by cutting a parchment circle to fit inside.

4 In a small bowl, combine graham cracker crumbs, sugar, and salt. Using a fork, stir in melted butter until well combined. Press mixture into prepared pan. Bake 10 minutes. Cool on a wire rack while you prepare filling.

5 To make filling: Decrease oven temperature to 325°. In an electric stand mixer fitted with the paddle attachment, beat cream cheese at medium-low speed until creamy, about 2 minutes. Scrape down sides of bowl. With mixer on low, gradually add sugar, then flour, and finally a pinch of salt. Scrape down sides again.

6 Switch to a whisk attachment and continue by mixing in vanilla, lemon juice, and lemon zest. Whip in eggs and yolk, one at a time, scraping bowl, and whisk at least twice. Continue to whip on low speed and add sour cream. Whip until will blended; do not overbeat. Batter should be light and somewhat airy.

7 Brush sides of springform pan with melted butter. Wrap outside of pan tightly in heavy-duty aluminum foil. Pour filling into pan. Place pan in large roasting pan and pour hot tap water into roaster so that it comes about halfway up springform pan. Transfer to oven and bake until filling is just set in center, about 45 minutes. If edges start to pull away from the sides of pan sooner than that, remove it from oven. Immediately remove pan from water and remove foil. Place on wire rack and cool to room temperature.

continued on next page

8 Stir lemon curd until smooth (it should be the consistency of thick sour cream) and spread over surface of cheesecake. Cover springform with plastic wrap and refrigerate 8 hours or overnight. To unmold cake, place a hot towel around pan to loosen cake from sides. Run a butter knife around edges and remove outer part of pan.

Makes 10 to 12 servings.

Cranberry Cobbler

Chef: Bill Telepan

Orange zest in the crust and the filling adds depth of flavor to this sophisticated yet unpretentious cobbler.

TOPPING

6 Tbsp. (³/₄ stick) unsalted butter, softened
½ cup sugar
2 large eggs
1 tsp. vanilla extract
1 tsp. freshly grated orange zest
1 cup all-purpose flour
1 tsp. baking powder
½ tsp. salt

FILLING

6 cups fresh cranberries
1 ¼ cups sugar
1 cup cranberry juice
1 tsp. freshly grated orange zest

1 Preheat oven to 350°. To make topping: In a large bowl, beat butter and sugar with a wooden spoon until smooth and creamy. Beat in eggs 1 at a time until well blended. Beat in vanilla extract and orange zest. Add flour, baking powder and salt, and beat until fully blended. Set aside.

2 To make filling: In a 2-quart shallow glass or ceramic baking dish, combine cranberries, sugar, juice, and orange zest.

3 Spoon topping over cranberry mixture by heaping tablespoonfuls. Bake 55 to 60 minutes, or until filling is bubbly around the edges and topping is brown. Cool on a wire rack. Serve warm or at room temperature.

Makes 6 to 8 servings.

Apple Pie

Created by Joyce Maynard

Apples, cinnamon, pie dough, and good friends are a perfect recipe.

FILLING

3 pounds (6 to 7 large) Granny Smith, Cortland, Empire, or McIntosh apples, peeled, cored, and cut into chunks

3/4 cup sugar

2 Tbsp. fresh lemon juice

1/2 tsp. ground cinnamon

CRUST

3 cups all-purpose flour

1/2 tsp. salt

1/2 cup Crisco vegetable shortening

1 stick plus 1 Tbsp. chilled butter, cut into pieces

1/3 to 1/2 cup ice water

2 Tbsp. Minute tapioca

1 Tbsp. milk or cream

1 Tbsp. sugar

1. To make the filling: In a large bowl, combine the apples, sugar, lemon juice, and cinnamon. Let stand, stirring occasionally.

2. Preheat the oven to 400°. To make the crust: In a large bowl, mix the flour and salt. Using a pastry blender, work in the shortening and 1 stick of butter until the mixture resembles coarse crumbs. Sprinkle 1 Tbsp. of the ice water over the flour mixture, stirring gently with a fork. Continue adding the water just until the dough holds together. Shape the dough into a ball and divide it into two discs, one slightly larger than the other.

3. Place the smaller disc on a sheet of waxed paper, and use a lightly floured rolling pin to roll the dough into a 12-inch circle. If the dough sticks to the rolling pin, dust it lightly with more flour. Lay a 9- to 10-inch pie pan face down on top of the circle; flip the pan over and remove the paper. For the top crust, on a sheet of waxed paper, roll out the other disc to form a 14-inch circle. (An alternative method is to roll out each disc between two sheets of waxed paper.) Do not roll the dough more than necessary.

4. Sprinkle the tapioca on the bottom crust. Add the filling, mounding it in the center, and dot with 1 Tbsp. butter. Lift the waxed paper with the remaining crust and flip it over the filling. Peel back waxed paper. Trim the edges of the crusts and pinch together the top and bottom crusts. Optional: Roll out the trimmings and cut into decorative shapes. Brush the pie with the milk, and arrange the shapes on the crust. Sprinkle with sugar. Poke fork holes or cut vents in the top crust. Bake 40 to 45 minutes, or until golden brown. Serve warm.

Makes 8 servings.

Vermont Maple Sugar Pie

Chef: Tom Bivins

Glazed and infused with homegrown maple syrup, this pie is an incredibly refined version of the classic New England dish.

CRUST

1 cup all-purpose flour

¾ tsp. granulated sugar

¼ tsp. salt

6 Tbsp. vegetable shortening

2 Tbsp. cold water

1 large egg yolk

¾ tsp. apple cider vinegar

FILLING

3 large eggs, lightly beaten

1 cup Vermont maple syrup

2 Tbsp. butter, melted and cooled

¼ cup firmly packed dark brown sugar

¼ cup Vermont maple sugar*

2 Tbsp. fresh lemon juice

2 Tbsp. all-purpose flour

1 tsp. pure vanilla extract

1 tsp. finely grated lemon zest

Pinch of salt

TOPPING

Ice cream or whipped cream (optional)

*Available at www.maplesyrupvermont.com.

1 Preheat oven to 375°. To make crust: In a large mixing bowl, blend together flour, sugar, and salt with a fork. Cut in shortening with a pastry cutter. In a small bowl, beat together water, egg yolk, and vinegar. Pour liquid over flour mixture and mix quickly with a fork (texture will be sticky). Using your hands, shape dough into a disc and refrigerate at least 1 hour.

2 Remove from refrigerator; roll dough on a floured surface into a 12-inch circle, about ⅛ inch thick. Place in a 9-inch pie dish and trim to 1 inch over the edge of the pan. Fold under and crimp edge with fingers to make a high fluted border. Chill at least 30 minutes.

3 To make filling: In a large bowl, whisk together all filling ingredients until smooth. Pour into chilled pie crust and bake about 35 minutes, or until edges are set but center jiggles slightly. Cool to room temperature on a wire rack. Serve with ice cream or whipped cream, if desired.

Makes 8 servings.

Sweet Potato & Pecan Pie with Cinnamon Cream

Chef: Govind Armstrong

Nothing says Southern hospitality better than this scrumptious pie.

TOPPING

1 egg

3 Tbsp. dark corn syrup

3 Tbsp. firmly packed light brown sugar

1 Tbsp. margarine or butter, melted

1 tsp. maple flavoring

1 cup chopped pecans

PIE

1 pound (2 medium) sweet potatoes, baked, peeled, and kept warm

¼ cup margarine or butter

One (14-ounce) can sweetened condensed milk

1 tsp. grated orange zest

1 tsp. vanilla extract

1 tsp. ground cinnamon

1 tsp. ground nutmeg

¼ tsp. kosher salt

2 eggs

One (9-inch) unbaked pastry shell

CINNAMON CREAM

1 cup heavy cream

½ tsp. ground cinnamon

3 Tbsp. granulated sugar

1 To make topping: In a small mixing bowl, combine egg, corn syrup, light brown sugar, margarine, and maple flavoring; mix well. Stir in pecans and set aside.

2 To make pie: Preheat oven to 350°. In a large mixing bowl, beat warm sweet potatoes with margarine until smooth. Add condensed milk, orange zest, vanilla, cinnamon, nutmeg, salt, and eggs; mix well. Pour into pastry shell. Bake 30 minutes. Remove from oven; spoon topping evenly over pie. Bake 20 to 25 minutes longer, or until golden brown. Cool. Serve warm or chilled.

3 To make cinnamon cream: In a medium-size bowl over ice, whisk heavy cream. Add cinnamon and sugar, and whisk to medium-stiff peaks. Serve alongside pie.

Makes 10 servings.

At the Table with Rozanne Gold
EVERY MEAL IS AN EVENT

What I can do with za'tar!" declares Rozanne Gold, the award-winning chef and cookbook author who has made a name for herself turning simplicity into an art form. "It's a spice mix I always have on hand. I love Middle Eastern flavors. If I heard a few people were stopping by in ten minutes, when they walked in I would offer them freshly baked triangles of pita bread spread with olive oil and sprinkled with za'tar, hot from the oven. So simple yet magical."

Rozanne is a trained chef who has directed her talents to consulting for restaurants and companies looking for innovation and spot-on conceptual thinking. She has written ten cookbooks and is at work on two more, including a book for teens and a large, ambitious collection of recipes called *The New Gold Standard*. She is perhaps best known for her 1-2-3 series of cookbooks, which present recipes that require only three ingredients.

The chef says that she lives and cooks simply. Her kitchen is without a dishwasher or microwave, featuring instead a battery of mix-and-match pots and a collection of top-notch knives. She loves to give what she calls "pots, pans, and platters" parties where many of the dishes are served straight from the cooking implement. This type of casual presentation makes people feel at ease, she says.

Rozanne is married to Michael Whiteman, and while the two are New York–based, internationally known restaurant consultants, they entertain at home often. "Our family is very small but we quickly become large when we invite our friends over," she says.

Dinner at their Brooklyn home is always an adventure because Rozanne believes in mixing it up so that every meal is an event and everyone learns something new. She once organized an upside-down wine meal,

> "Our family is very small but we quickly become large when we invite our friends over."

where the first course was accompanied by dessert wine and dessert was served with a cocktail. The courses in between were suitably paired with wines in a backward progression and the result was a giddy education for everyone. Another evening she might arrange a Hungarian night, replete with comfort foods from her childhood when her Hungarian mother cooked cabbage and noodles or molded a meatloaf in the shape of a heart.

For me, cooking and entertaining are all about the emotional connection," Rozanne says. "I call special touches 'grace notes,' and without them, the meal is not worth cooking. Recently I made a red tomato–watermelon gazpacho and a green Asian gazpacho, each served in tiny shot glasses so that my guests got two glasses. I also like to end a meal with homemade ice cream and a giant, ultrathin cookie that I put in the center of the table and everyone breaks off pieces." And she never lets guests leave her home without something small from the kitchen, like her signature Venetian Wine Cake, wrapped in colorful cellophane.

Creativity—in and outside the kitchen—and caring about those who gather around her table are Rozanne's trademarks. Her concept of embellishing every meal with simple grace notes is one that plays anywhere, anytime.

Rozanne Gold's Recipes
- **Heirloom Tomatoes with Lemon Tahini** (page 26)
- **Watermelon Lemonade** (page 50)
- **Seared Tuna with Fresh Corn & Wasabi "Cream"** (page 142)
- **Salt-Roasted Yukon Gold Potatoes with Bay Leaves** (page 184)

Carrot Cake with Soy Cream Cheese Frosting

Chef: Rori Trovato

The addition of pineapple lends tang to this crumbly carrot cake.

This recipe requires parchment paper and two 9-inch cake pans.

CAKE

2 ½ cups all-purpose flour, plus more for dusting

1 tsp. baking powder

1 tsp. kosher salt

¼ tsp. ground nutmeg

2 tsp. ground cinnamon

2 tsp. baking soda

4 large eggs

½ cup honey, slightly warmed

1 cup firmly packed light brown sugar

1 cup vegetable oil

1 cup crushed pineapple (fresh or canned), plus ¼ cup juice

1 Tbsp. vanilla extract

3 cups shredded carrots, loosely packed

1 cup chopped walnuts

1 cup shredded coconut, preferably unsweetened

1 cup raisins

FROSTING

Two (18-ounce) containers soy cream cheese, chilled

¾ cup firmly packed light brown sugar

1 ½ tsp. vanilla extract

247

1 To make cake: Preheat oven to 350°. Grease two 9-inch cake pans with vegetable cooking oil spray, line bottoms with parchment paper, and grease the paper. Dust with flour and shake off excess. Set aside.

2 Combine flour, baking powder, salt, nutmeg, cinnamon, and baking soda in a mixing bowl. In a medium bowl, beat eggs, honey, and brown sugar with a wooden spoon until well combined. Stir in vegetable oil, pineapple juice, and vanilla until well combined. Add flour mixture and stir until well combined. Fold in the pineapple, carrots, nuts, coconut, and raisins; mix until well blended.

3 To make frosting: With an electric mixer, beat soy cream cheese until fluffy, about 2 minutes. Add brown sugar and vanilla, and beat 2 more minutes.

4 Place one layer on a cake plate. Coat top with about ½ cup frosting, and place second layer on top of the first. Frost sides of entire cake before frosting the top. Refrigerate until ready to serve.

Makes one 9-inch 2-layer cake.

Fig Galette

Chef: Colleen McGlynn

A rustic fig galette with a free-form crust is filled with
fruit that promises a burst of intense flavor.

PASTRY

1 ½ cups all-purpose flour

2 Tbsp. sugar

1 Tbsp. cornmeal

½ tsp. salt

1 ½ sticks (12 Tbsp.) butter, cut into
  ½-inch pieces and kept cold

6 or 7 Tbsp. ice water

FILLING

⅓ cup sugar

2 baskets (about 1 ½ pounds) fresh figs

Whipped cream (optional)

1 To make pastry: Combine flour, sugar, cornmeal, and salt in a large bowl. With pastry blender or two knives used scissors fashion, cut in butter until mixture resembles fine crumbs. Add ice water, 1 Tbsp. at a time, mixing lightly with a fork until pastry is moist enough to hold together and begins to come away from sides of bowl. Form dough into a disc and wrap tightly in plastic. Refrigerate at least 1 hour or overnight.

2 Preheat oven to 375°. Line a large cookie sheet with parchment paper. Roll out dough on a lightly floured surface; shape into a 14-inch circle. Transfer to prepared sheet.

3 To make filling: Sprinkle top of dough with half of sugar. Trim stems from figs and cut each lengthwise into 4 or 5 slices. Arrange figs on pastry in concentric circles, slightly overlapping and with a 2-inch border around edge. Sprinkle fruit with remaining sugar. Lift pastry edge and fold over filling to make a pleated border.

4 Bake tart 45 to 50 minutes, until fruit is bubbling and edges are golden. Remove from oven and allow to cool at least 30 minutes. Top with whipped cream, if desired.

Makes 8 servings.

Blueberry Buckle

Chefs: Melissa Kelly and Price Kushner

This homespun dish is a variation on the traditional American classic.

CRUMBLE
¼ cup granulated sugar
¼ cup dark brown sugar, packed
½ cup all-purpose flour
⅛ tsp. ground cinnamon
4 Tbsp. butter, cold

BATTER
4 Tbsp. butter
5 Tbsp. granulated sugar
1 egg
1 cup flour
1 tsp. baking soda
½ cup buttermilk

FILLING
4 cups (2 pints) blueberries
1 Tbsp. fresh lemon juice
1 Tbsp. flour
2 to 4 Tbsp. granulated sugar

1 To prepare crumble: Combine all ingredients in a large bowl and break apart with fingers. Refrigerate.

2 To prepare batter: In a medium-size bowl, cream butter and sugar, then mix in egg. Sift together dry ingredients. Add half the dry ingredients to the creamed butter; mix, then add buttermilk; mix, then add remaining dry ingredients; mix just to combine. Refrigerate batter 30 minutes.

3 To prepare filling: Combine all ingredients in a bowl; stir.

4 Grease eight 6-ounce ramekins or soufflé dishes (or one large Pyrex pie pan). Add ¼ cup batter to each mold, smoothing mixture with a plastic spatula. Add ½ cup blueberries, then top each with ¼ cup crumble. Bake at 350° for 30 to 35 minutes, until top is browned and filling just starts to bubble. Remove from oven and allow to cool 20 minutes. Serve warm or at room temperature.

Makes 8 servings.

250

Bittersweet Chocolate Basil Tart with Honey Grapefruit Sauce

Chef: Debra Ponzek

The sauce is a zesty complement to the tart's rich chocolate filling.

TART SHELL

6 Tbsp. (³⁄₄ stick) butter, softened
¼ cup granulated sugar
1 ¼ cups cake flour (not self-rising)
1 egg

FILLING

1 cup heavy cream
⅓ cup whole milk
½ cup finely shredded basil leaves, loosely packed
8 ounces bittersweet chocolate, chopped
1 egg

GARNISH

Confectioners' sugar
Fresh basil sprig

SAUCE

3 pink grapefruits, peeled and cut into segments, saving juice
3 Tbsp. honey
1 ½ tsp. cornstarch mixed with 2 tsp. water

1 To make tart shell: In the bowl of an electric mixer fitted with a paddle attachment, beat butter and granulated sugar until light and fluffy. With mixer on low speed, add flour and egg in two parts and beat just until combined. Shape dough into a disc, wrap in waxed paper, and chill 1 to 24 hours. Roll out dough on a lightly floured surface with a lightly floured rolling pin to ⅛- to ¼-inch thickness. Transfer to a 9-inch tart pan, press in sides and bottom, and trim any excess dough around edges. Preheat oven to 350°. Cover dough with a large piece of foil and weigh down with uncooked rice or beans. Bake 20 minutes, remove foil and beans, and bake 10 minutes longer, or until light golden brown. Cool on a rack.

2 To make filling, preheat oven to 375°. In a medium saucepan over medium heat, bring cream, milk, and basil just to a boil. Remove pan from heat, cover, and steep 10 minutes.

3 Place chocolate in a medium bowl. Pour cream mixture through a strainer over chocolate and whisk until smooth. Let cool 10 minutes, then whisk in egg.

4 Pour chocolate into tart shell and bake 20 minutes, or until filling is just beginning to set.

5 Remove to a wire rack and let cool completely. Dust with confectioners' sugar and garnish with basil sprig.

6 Meanwhile, to make sauce: Chop grapefruit segments into small pieces, saving juice. In a medium saucepan over medium heat, bring fruit, reserved juices, and honey to a boil. Add cornstarch mixture and boil 1 minute, or until slightly thickened. Remove from heat, transfer to a bowl, and let cool to room temperature. Serve with tart (or with lemon cake).

Makes 20 servings.

252

Banoffee Tart

Chef: April Bloomfield

Turn condensed milk, bananas, and whipped cream—with a
sprinkle of bittersweet chocolate—into pure heaven.

FILLING AND TART SHELL

Two (14-ounce) cans sweetened
  condensed milk
2 cups all-purpose flour
2/3 cup confectioners' sugar
1/2 tsp. kosher salt
1 1/2 sticks cold unsalted butter, cut
  into 1/2-inch cubes
2 large egg yolks, lightly beaten
9 to 10 bananas

TOPPING

2 cups heavy cream
3 Tbsp. confectioners' sugar
1 vanilla bean, split lengthwise
Grated bittersweet chocolate, for
  garnish

1 To make filling: Preheat oven to 425°. Bring a pot of water to a boil. Pour condensed milk into a 9-inch deep-dish glass pie plate. Cover with foil. Place pie plate in a large roasting pan and place pan on center oven rack. Pour boiling water into roasting pan halfway up sides of pie plate. Bake 2 hours, whisking milk 2 times, until thickened and caramel colored. Remove pie plate to wire rack. Whisk milk until smooth, and let cool.

2 To make tart shell: Lower oven temperature to 300°.
In the bowl of a heavy-duty mixer with paddle attached, mix flour, sugar, and salt on low speed until blended. Add butter and blend until mixture is the texture of fine meal. With mixer running, drizzle in egg yolks and mix until dough begins to come together. Gather dough into a ball and flatten into a disc. Wrap and freeze until firm, about 40 minutes.

3 Cut dough into 4 pieces. Using the large holes of a box grater, grate dough into an 11-inch tart pan with removable bottom. Press dough firmly and evenly against sides and bottom of pan. Prick bottom with a fork. Freeze 15 minutes.

4 Line tart shell with foil and fill with dried beans or rice. Bake tart shell in lower third of oven 30 minutes. Remove foil and beans. Return to oven and bake until golden brown, 25 to 30 minutes. If shell puffs up during baking, press it down with the back of a spoon. Remove to rack to cool.

5 Peel and thinly slice bananas. Arrange half of bananas in concentric circles, slightly overlapping, to cover bottom of tart shell. Spoon on caramelized milk and spread to cover bananas. Arrange remaining bananas over milk. Cover tart with plastic wrap, pressing wrap against bananas, and refrigerate 1 hour.

6 To make topping: In the bowl of a heavy-duty mixer with whisk attachment, combine cream and sugar. Using a paring knife, scrape seeds from vanilla bean into cream. Beat mixture until just stiff. Spread over bananas and sprinkle with grated chocolate.

Makes 12 servings.

Pumpkin & Blueberry Tart

Chef: Michel Nischan

You may not think of combining such distinct flavors,
but they prove to be a stunning match.

PASTRY

10 ½ Tbsp. unsalted butter

1 ½ cups all-purpose flour, plus more
for dusting

3 Tbsp. raw sugar

¼ tsp. salt

1 large egg, beaten

FILLING

2 cups preserved pumpkin or
pumpkin pie filling

½ tsp. ground cinnamon

2 ½ cups fresh blueberries

¼ cup local honey

¼ vanilla bean, split

1 Tbsp. chopped fresh mint leaves

1 mint sprig, for garnish

1 To make pastry: Place butter in freezer for 15 minutes. In a large bowl, whisk flour, sugar, and salt to combine. Using the large holes of a grater, grate butter into flour mixture; combine until they form a coarse meal. Drizzle with egg, and stir with a fork until dough forms. Shape dough into a ball, then divide into 4 equal pieces. Place each portion of dough on a lightly floured work surface and flatten with the palm of your hand to blend; gather dough up and repeat. Gather all dough together into a ball and press into a disc; wrap and refrigerate until firm enough to roll, about 30 minutes.

2 On a lightly floured work surface, with a floured rolling pin, roll dough into a 13-inch circle. Drape dough over rolling pin and ease into an 11-inch tart pan with removable bottom. Gently press dough against sides of pan and trim excess by running rolling pin over rim; refrigerate 20 minutes.

3 Preheat oven to 475°. Line tart shell with foil and fill with dried beans or pie weights. Bake until edge begins to brown, about 15 minutes. Remove foil and beans. Bake until bottom of shell is golden brown, 3 to 5 minutes; let cool on rack 15 minutes.

4 To make filling: Reduce oven temperature to 350°. Spoon pumpkin into tart shell and spread evenly. Sprinkle with cinnamon and top with blueberries in a single layer. Bake 6 to 7 minutes; let cool.

5 In a microwaveproof bowl, combine honey, vanilla bean, and mint. Microwave on high until just warm, about 15 minutes. Strain honey through a fine sieve set over a bowl. Right before serving, drizzle honey over tart and garnish with mint.

Makes 10 servings.

Tiramisu

Chef: Pino Coladonato

This famous Italian dessert is made from biscuits with coffee, cocoa, and mascarpone cream. A splash of brandy is the special touch here.

5 pasteurized eggs, separated
1 cup sugar
3 Tbsp. brandy
1 pound mascarpone
2 Tbsp. coffee liqueur
1 cup espresso, chilled
1 Tbsp. cocoa powder
14 ounces ladyfingers

1 Using an electric mixer, beat the yolks, sugar, and 1 Tbsp. of the brandy until sugar dissolves. Beat in the mascarpone, and set aside the mixture in the refrigerator.

2 Beat the egg whites until they form soft peaks. Gently fold the whites into the mascarpone mixture.

3 Add the coffee liqueur and the remaining 2 Tbsp. of brandy to the espresso.

4 Spread a third of the mascarpone mixture in the bottom of a 9" x 13" glass baking dish and dust lightly with cocoa powder. Next, generously brush the ladyfingers with espresso and lay enough of them side by side to cover the mascarpone and cocoa. Repeat with a second layer of one-third of the mascarpone, a dusting of cocoa, and more ladyfingers. Top with the remaining ⅓ pound of the mascarpone and dust with the remaining cocoa. Cover dish with plastic wrap. Refrigerate for a minimum of 12 hours.

Makes 16 servings.

256

Pumpkin Fritters with Vanilla Ice Cream

Chef: Colin Cowie

These crunchy little fritters are marvelously tempting, delightfully crisp, and just a little bit fragile.

½ cup all-purpose flour

3 to 4 Tbsp. granulated sugar

2 tsp. baking powder

1 tsp. ground cinnamon

½ tsp. salt

2 large eggs

One (15-ounce) can 100 percent pure pumpkin

Canola or vegetable oil, for frying

Cinnamon sugar (see step 4)

Vanilla ice cream, for serving

1 Line a baking sheet with paper toweling and set aside. In a small bowl, stir together flour, sugar, baking powder, cinnamon, and salt. In a medium bowl, whisk eggs until blended. Whisk in pumpkin until combined.

2 Frying 4 at a time, drop batter by heaping (measuring) table-spoonfuls into pan. Fry until golden brown, turning occasionally, about 4 minutes. Using slotted spoon, transfer fritters to paper towels to drain. Repeat with remaining batter. Fritters will puff up, then deflate slightly when removed from pan. To test for doneness, press lightly on fritters; they should spring back.

3 To serve, arrange fritters (2 each) on small dessert plates. Sprinkle each with slightly rounded teaspoon cinnamon sugar and serve with ice cream.

4 To make cinnamon sugar: In a small dish, stir together 3 tablespoons sugar and 1 table-spoon cinnamon until combined.

Makes 10 servings (about 20 fritters).

Traditional Pavlova

Created by Mimi Pond

This meringue shell filled with whipped cream and topped with summer fruits draws "oohs" and "aahs" but is so easy to prepare.

½ cup superfine sugar

1 Tbsp. cornstarch

4 large egg whites, room temperature

¼ tsp. salt

¼ tsp. cream of tartar

1 tsp. vanilla

1 tsp. white vinegar

1 cup whipping cream

2 pints mixed berries (strawberries, raspberries, blueberries)

1 Preheat oven to 275°. Line a cookie sheet with foil or parchment paper. Using a 10-inch round cake pan or plate as a guide, lightly trace a circle (use a toothpick on foil or a pencil on parchment). Set aside.

2 In a small bowl, combine ¼ cup sugar and the cornstarch. Mix with a fork until smooth.

3 With a mixer on high speed, beat egg whites to a foam and add salt and the cream of tartar. Continue to beat until soft peaks form. Gradually add the remaining ¼ cup sugar, 2 Tbsp. at a time, while beating constantly, until peaks stiffen. Beat in the cornstarch mixture until just blended. Add the vanilla and vinegar, continuing to mix until just blended. Spoon the mixture onto the cookie sheet. Using the circle of paper as a guide, spread the meringue into a large "nest," using the back of a tablespoon (the edges should be 1½ inches high, and the center should be shallow). Bake for 1 hour and 15 minutes. Turn the heat off and leave the meringue in the oven for 1 hour to dry thoroughly. Remove and cool completely on a wire rack.

4 Peel the paper from the bottom of the meringue, and place the dessert on a serving dish or cake plate. Just before serving, whip the cream into soft peaks and spoon into the center of the meringue. Top the whipped cream with the fruit and serve immediately.

Serves 8.

Chocolate Pots de Crème with Vanilla Ice Cream

Chef: Colin Cowie

Another dessert that looks elaborate but can be prepared and chilled well in advance.

4 ounces good-quality bittersweet or semisweet chocolate. coarsely chopped
1 cup heavy or whipping cream
½ cup milk
4 large egg yolks
¼ cup sugar
½ pint fresh raspberries
1 quart vanilla ice cream

1 Place chocolate in a medium bowl. In a small saucepan, bring cream and milk just to a boil. Add to chocolate; whisk until mixture is smooth and chocolate is melted. Refrigerate 30 minutes.

2 Meanwhile, preheat oven to 350°. Place 10 espresso (or other small) cups in a large roasting pan.

3 In a large bowl, whisk together egg yolks and sugar until blended but not foamy. Gradually whisk in chocolate mixture until blended. Strain custard through a 1-quart sieve set over a large glass measuring cup.

4 Pour a scant ¼ cup custard into each espresso cup. Place pan with cups on center oven rack; carefully pour enough hot water into pan so it reaches halfway up sides of cups. Bake until custards are set in the center, 35 to 40 minutes. Transfer custards to a cooling rack; cool to room temperature, then refrigerate at least 1 hour. Top with raspberries and ice cream.

Makes 10 servings.

261

Banana Pudding

Created by Maya Angelou

Serve this meringue-topped pudding the next time you invite friends for dinner. It's both elegant and totally irresistible.

¾ cup plus 1 Tbsp. sugar
⅓ cup cornstarch
Pinch of salt
3 cups milk
8 eggs, separated
3 Tbsp. butter
1 Tbsp. pure vanilla extract
3 cups vanilla wafers
4 ripe bananas, thinly sliced
½ tsp. cream of tartar

1 Preheat oven to 350°. In a large saucepan, combine ⅓ cup sugar, cornstarch, and salt; stir until blended. Mix in milk. Cook over medium heat, stirring constantly, until thickened and boiling. Boil 1 minute, then remove from heat.

2 In a small bowl, whisk egg yolks, then whisk in about ½ cup of hot custard until blended. Pour yolk mixture back into saucepan of custard; cook over medium heat, stirring, 2 minutes. Stir in butter and vanilla until blended.

3 Place vanilla wafers on bottom of a shallow 2-quart casserole dish. Top with layer of banana slices and custard. Repeat layering, ending with custard.

4 In a large mixing bowl, beat egg whites and ¼ cup sugar at low speed until frothy. Add cream of tartar, increase speed to medium, and gradually beat in remaining sugar. Beat until egg whites hold stiff peaks.

5 Spoon meringue over hot custard immediately, making sure that meringue touches baking dish on all sides (this prevents it from shrinking). Transfer to oven and bake until golden, about 20 minutes. Remove pudding from oven and cool 1 hour. Refrigerate at least 4 hours before serving.

Makes 8 servings.

Spice-Dusted Brownies

Chef: Alice Medrich

These brownies are wizardly and so rich, you'll feel guilty eating
more than one (which shouldn't stop you).

BROWNIE

8 ounces bittersweet (70 percent)
   chocolate

6 Tbsp. unsalted butter

2 large eggs

1 cup sugar

1 tsp. pure vanilla extract

¼ tsp. salt

¼ cup all-purpose flour

CRUST

1 stick unsalted butter, melted

¼ cup sugar

¼ tsp. vanilla extract

¼ tsp. salt

1 cup all-purpose flour

⅔ cup coarsely chopped walnuts

1 cup chilled crème fraîche, for
   topping*

Whole nutmeg

*If you can't find crème fraîche in your
local market, substitute sour cream,
unsweetened whipped cream, or a
mixture of both. Crème fraîche is similar
to sour cream but lighter and milder.

1 Position a rack in the lower
third of the oven; preheat oven
to 350°. Line bottom and sides of
an 8-inch-square baking pan with
foil, and set aside.

2 To make brownie: Place chocolate and butter in top of a double
boiler over almost-simmering water.
Stir frequently until chocolate is
melted and mixture is smooth and
very warm to touch.

3 Remove from heat and set
aside. In a medium bowl, beat
eggs, sugar, vanilla, and salt at high
speed with an electric mixer until
mixture is thick and light in color,
3 to 4 minutes. Stir in flour. Scrape
in warm chocolate mixture and
fold with a rubber spatula until
just combined. Set aside until
needed.

4 To make crust: In a medium
bowl, combine melted butter,
sugar, vanilla, and salt. Stir in flour,
then walnut pieces. Turn out into
pan; press dough evenly across
bottom. Bake until crust is fully
golden brown, 15 to 20 minutes.

5 Remove pan from oven, but
leave oven on. Scrape brownie
batter onto hot crust and spread
evenly, swirling surface. Return to
oven and bake just until a toothpick inserted in two or three
places comes out clean, 20 to 22
minutes. Set pan on a rack to cool.
(If serving brownies warm, cool
just long enough to remove from
pan without cracking.) To remove
brownies from pan, lift edges of
foil. Transfer to a cutting board.
Gently slide a thin spatula
between crust and foil; slide
brownies off foil.

6 To serve, cut with a heavy
knife. Whip crème fraîche
just until it holds its shape. Divide
brownies among serving plates and
grate nutmeg over brownies (use a
Microplane or nutmeg grater to
get the topping just right). Top
with a dollop of crème fraîche
and a little more grated nutmeg.

Makes 16 large or 25 small brownies.

Black Currant Tea–Chocolate Truffles

Chef: Mary Jo Thoresen

These are far easier to make than you might think and are a thoughtful and impressive housewarming gift.

½ cup plus 1 Tbsp. crème fraîche
1 Tbsp. plus 1 tsp. unsalted butter
½ ounce black currant tea (approximately 2 Tbsp. loose tea or tea leaves from 6 tea bags)
10 ounces semisweet chocolate, finely chopped
Unsweetened cocoa

1 In a small saucepan, combine crème fraîche, butter, and 2 Tbsp. water. Bring to a boil. Remove from heat and add tea. Cover and let steep 5 minutes. Strain mixture through a fine sieve into a clean saucepan.

2 Put chocolate into a medium-size bowl. Bring crème fraîche mixture to a boil again and pour over chocolate. Stir gently until all chocolate is melted (do not whisk). Pour into a 9-inch baking pan and spread evenly. Chill until firm.

3 Line a cookie sheet with waxed paper. Using a melon baller, scoop chocolate to form balls about ¾ inch in diameter, then roll gently into balls using palms. When rolling truffles, you can wear vinyl or latex gloves, or use your bare hands, if you dust your palms with cocoa powder. Without gloves the rolling will be easier, but not less messy. Place truffles on lined cookie sheet; cover and chill just to set, about 1 hour.

4 To serve, place cocoa in a pie pan. Add several truffles one at a time to cocoa and swirl pan to coat. Transfer to serving plate or place truffles in mini muffin cups (available at grocery stores).

Makes about 2 dozen.

266

Lemon Honey Sherbet

Created by Susan Chumsky

Honey adds a gorgeous sweetness not just to food but to life.

2 tsp. unflavored gelatin
¾ cup honey
1 cup fresh lemon juice
1 ½ cups plain organic yogurt
½ cup whole milk

1 Place 2 Tbsp. water in a small bowl and sprinkle with gelatin. Set aside until spongy, about 5 minutes. Meanwhile, in a small saucepan, heat honey with ¼ cup water over medium heat until honey is dissolved. Remove from heat and let sit 1 minute. Add gelatin and stir until dissolved. Cool to room temperature, then stir in lemon juice. Chill 30 minutes in refrigerator.

2 Using an electric ice cream maker, churn until thickened but not thick enough to scoop. Add yogurt and milk and continue to churn, 15 to 20 minutes. Remove and place in a freezeproof container; freeze until firm.

Makes 4 to 6 servings.

268

Heavenly Fresh Mint Ice Cream

Created by Peggy Knickerbocker

This easy ice cream is even more delicious topped with berries or sliced peaches.

2 cups (1 pint) heavy cream
1 cup whole milk
12 large fresh mint sprigs, coarsely torn
7 large egg yolks
¾ cup sugar

1 In a medium-heavy saucepan, bring cream and milk to a boil. Remove from heat. Add mint sprigs, cover pot, and allow to steep 30 minutes. Pour mixture through a fine-mesh sieve into a medium bowl; discard solids.

2 In a small bowl, whisk together egg yolks and sugar until thick and pale. Add a few Tbsp. warm milk mixture to egg mixture, whisking vigorously. Once combined, add egg mixture back into milk mixture, whisking continuously.

3 Return to saucepan; cook over medium-low heat, stirring constantly with a large heatproof rubber spatula, until custard thickens enough to coat the back of a spoon (a mark should remain when you can run your finger down spoon). Alternatively, cook until an instant thermometer reads 175° to 180°. Do not allow mixture to boil.

4 Strain custard through a fine-mesh sieve into a glass bowl; discard solids. Cover and refrigerate at least 1 hour or up to 1 day. (To quicken chilling time, place glass bowl in a larger bowl filled with ice water until custard thickens slightly and is completely cool to touch.)

5 Freeze custard according to ice cream maker instructions. Transfer to airtight container and freeze up to 2 days, removing ice cream from freezer about 10 minutes before serving to soften. Or serve immediately after making.

Makes about 1 quart.

Sour Cream Ice Cream with Caramelized Pear Compote

Created by Gale Gand

Why make your own when you can open a pint? Because homemade ice cream is among life's supreme pleasures.

ICE CREAM

1 container (16 ounces) sour cream

1 cup plus 2 Tbsp. sugar

1 cup half-and-half

2 Tbsp. fresh lemon juice

¼ tsp. salt

Vanilla bean, split open (or ½ tsp. vanilla extract)

PEAR COMPOTE

4 Tbsp. (½ stick) unsalted butter

½ cup sugar

1 cinnamon stick (optional)

2 tsp. brandy

1 tsp. fresh lemon juice

3 large, firm-ripe Bartlett pears, peeled, cored, and thinly sliced

1 To make ice cream: In a large bowl, whisk sour cream, sugar, half-and-half, lemon juice, and salt until blended. Scrape vanilla bean seeds into mixture and whisk until blended. Cover and refrigerate until well chilled, about 1 hour, or overnight.

2 Freeze sour cream mixture in an ice cream maker according to manufacturer's directions. In the meantime, place an 8-cup storage container in freezer. When ice cream is done, scoop into container and freeze at least 4 hours or overnight, until solid.

3 To make compote: In a large skillet, melt butter over medium heat. Stir in sugar and cinnamon stick, if using. Cook, stirring frequently, until sugar mixture turns caramel color, 3 to 5 minutes. Using a long-handled spoon, carefully stir in brandy and lemon juice (mixture will spatter). Add pears and cook, gently stirring

occasionally, until pears are tender and juices thicken slightly, 8 to 10 minutes. Remove and discard cinnamon stick.

4 To serve, scoop about ½ cup ice cream into each of 8 dessert bowls and top with warm pear compote. The ice cream recipe makes more than is needed for the dessert. In an airtight container, cover surface of leftover ice cream with plastic wrap, seal, and freeze for up to 1 week.

Makes 8 servings.

Grown-Up Milk & Cookies

Chef: Michelle Myers

A warm, bittersweet chocolate soufflé with a melted ganache center
is accompanied by a shot glass of milky eau-de-vie.

GANACHE CENTER
²⁄₃ cup heavy cream
Scant ¼ cup ground coffee
4 ounces bittersweet chocolate,
   coarsely chopped
3 Tbsp. unsalted butter, softened

COOKIE BATTER
⅓ cup almond meal or almond flour
3 large eggs, separated
Pinch of salt
¾ cup sugar
6 Tbsp. unsalted butter, melted
8 ounces bittersweet chocolate,
   melted
⅓ cup uncooked Cream of Wheat
¾ cup finely chopped toasted cocoa
   nibs (cocoa beans broken into small
   pieces)

MILK EAU-DE-VIE
2 cups whole milk
3 Tbsp. sugar
½ vanilla bean, split
2 Tbsp. eau-de-vie or grappa
Sugared cocoa nibs, for garnish

1 To make ganache: In a small saucepan, combine cream, ¼ cup water, and ground coffee. Heat over medium heat until hot. Remove from heat; let stand 15 minutes. Strain cream mixture through a fine sieve into a clean 2-quart saucepan. Heat cream mixture over medium heat and bring just to a boil; remove from heat.

2 Meanwhile, in a food processor with metal blade attached, finely chop chocolate. With motor running, pour hot cream mixture through feed cylinder. Add butter, and process until chocolate and butter are melted. Line a 9-inch-square baking pan with aluminum foil or plastic wrap, letting foil extend at two sides. Pour ganache into pan. Freeze until firm, about 1 hour.

3 To make cookie batter: Spray eight 3¼- to 3½-inch ramekins with cooking spray. Line bottoms with parchment circles, and spray again.

4 In a medium skillet over medium heat, cook almond meal until lightly toasted and fragrant, stirring frequently, about 5 minutes. Turn meal onto a plate to cool.

5 In a medium bowl, beat egg whites and salt with an electric mixer on medium-high speed until soft peaks begin to form. Shift mixer to high and gradually beat in sugar until whites stiffen.

6 In a large bowl, combine almond meal, egg yolks, melted butter, melted chocolate, Cream of Wheat, and cocoa nibs; stir until blended. Fold in egg whites. Spoon mixture into a large food storage bag and snip a large hole in one corner. Pipe mixture into bottom of ramekins to cover, about ½ inch thick.

7 Remove ganache from the freezer; lift from pan using foil ends. With a 2¼-inch round cutter, cut out 8 circles. Place a circle in the center of each ramekin. Pipe remaining batter over and around ganache to cover. Smooth tops. Freeze until firm, about 1 hour.

8 To make milk eau-de-vie: In a medium saucepan over medium-high heat, combine milk, sugar, and vanilla bean. Bring just to a boil, lower heat, and simmer until reduced to 1½ cups, about 15 minutes. Discard vanilla bean, pour milk into a bowl, and refrigerate until cold.

continued on next page

continued from previous page

9 Preheat oven to 375°. Place ramekins on a baking sheet and bake until tops feel firm, 21 to 23 minutes. Allow to cool on the baking sheet 10 minutes.

10 Place remaining ganache in a small saucepan and melt over low heat. To serve, run a knife carefully around the insides of the ramekins and invert cookies onto a plate. Remove paper. Drizzle with warm ganache and sugared cocoa nibs. Pour eau-de-vie and milk into shot glasses. Serve with cookies.

Makes 8 servings.

Port-Glazed Figs with Walnuts & Stilton

Chef: Rori Trovato

A meal that ends with port-glazed figs, walnuts, and Stilton is a meal that probably shouldn't end.

2 Tbsp. butter
½ cup walnut halves
¾ cup ruby port
12 small ripe figs (Mission, Kadota, Calimyrna, or Brown Turkey), trimmed and halved lengthwise
6-ounce wedge Stilton cheese, cut into 4 equal pieces

1 In a 10-inch skillet, melt butter over medium heat. Add walnuts and cook, stirring constantly, until lightly browned, 4 to 5 minutes. Using a slotted spoon, transfer walnuts to a bowl.

2 Add port to the warm skillet. Increase heat to high and boil until thickened, 4 to 5 minutes. Remove from heat and gently toss figs and walnuts in port syrup.

3 Place each piece of cheese on a separate plate. Top with fig and nut mixture and drizzle with any extra syrup. Serve immediately.

Makes 4 servings.

Summer Berry Pudding

Created by Moira Hodgson

Delight your taste buds with this decadent mélange
of fresh fruit and sweet spongy bread.

3 cups raspberries, plus more for
   garnish
½ cup sugar, or more to taste
1 ½ cups blackberries, blueberries, or
   black currants (or any combination
   of the three), stems removed, plus
   more for garnish
1 loaf firm white bread, sliced*
Mint sprigs, for garnish (optional)
Whipped cream, crème fraîche, or
   clotted cream

*Choosing a dense white sandwich
loaf such as Thomas's English Muffin
Toasting Bread or Pepperidge Farm
Toasting White Bread is crucial; light
packaged white breads won't hold
the shape.

1 Place raspberries in a stainless
steel saucepan; add 4 tablespoons sugar. Toss gently to combine. Bring to a boil. Taste (carefully—they're hot), and add more
sugar if necessary. Because the
sweetness of fresh fruit fluctuates,
don't follow the amount of sugar
blindly. Taste as you go. Cook 3 to
4 minutes, or until berries begin to
burst and yield more of their juice.
In a separate saucepan, combine
blackberries, blueberries, and/or
black currants; add 4 tablespoons
sugar. Toss gently and bring mixture briefly to a boil, as instructed
above. Taste, and add more sugar if
necessary.

2 Remove crusts from bread
slices. Using a downturned cup
as a template, cut one slice in
a circle and place it at the bottom
of a three-quart ceramic or glass
bowl. Line bottom and sides of
bowl with remaining bread slices,
cutting some in half or into shapes
as needed to cover any gaps where
fruit could run out. Do not over-
lap. Put a layer of raspberry mixture in, then a layer of blackberry
mixture, alternating until both are
gone, reserving 1 cup raspberry
juice. The bowl should be filled
with fruit almost to the rim.

3 Cover top with remaining
bread slices and press down
until they absorb the juices. Cover
with a saucer or plate that has a
diameter just smaller than the
diameter of the bowl, so that the
plate fits just inside the bowl.
Weight the plate with a heavy can.
Alternatively, place pudding in
refrigerator and wedge an object
snugly between the refrigerator
rack and the top of the plate so
that it pushes down on the pudding, achieving the same result as
the weight. Refrigerate overnight.

4 About 15 minutes before serving, remove pudding from
refrigerator. Remove can and
plate. Using a flexible, dull-edged
knife or spatula, loosen bread
around edges of bowl. Cover bowl
with a serving plate and, holding
the plate in place, turn the pudding
upside down. The bread should
have turned a deep ruby red. If
there are any light patches, pour
reserved raspberry juice over them.
Garnish with fresh berries and
mint sprigs, if you like. Serve with
whipped cream, crème fraîche, or
clotted cream on the side.

Makes 8 servings.

At the Table with Maya Angelou
THE JOYS OF COOKING

Almost every evening, says Maya Angelou, friends drop by about dinner time. "I wonder why?" she says with a smile and that famous laugh. There is no mystery, of course, because Dr. Angelou is known for her good cooking and expansive hospitality, which means there are always people around her table.

"You feel special when you cook for others," she says. "And you feel special when it's done for you."

Dr. Angelou, one of the country's most distinguished poets and writers, was asked to write a poem and then read it at the 1993 inauguration of President Bill Clinton. She is also the author of a book, *Hallelujah! The Welcome Table: A Lifetime of Memories with Recipes,* a collection of vignettes about her life and its accompanying dishes. First published in 2004, it was recently issued in paperback.

"I learned to cook by observing my mother and grandmother," she says of her Stamps, Arkansas, childhood. "I was a Depression baby and we were told to eat everything on our plates because of the little children starving in China. No one mentioned the little children starving right here in the United States."

Because of her upbringing, she learned to respect food as something greater than a source of nourishment. First, she found pleasure in experimenting with the creative component of cooking, marvelling at the fact that two or three ingredients, mixed together in a certain way, made an entirely new thing. "Every ingredient is important," she says.

She also learned about food's restorative powers. "I am convinced that if you have a rift with someone dear to you, if you want to ameliorate a fragile situation, food can help."

But food, for Dr. Angelou, is much more than a way to soothe discord. It's a joyful part of life. "My mother cooked a dish called Spanish rice," she recollects. It's a simple dish of rice cooked with sautéed onions, garlic, green bell peppers, and tomato sauce, and served with chicken. "When my mother invited me over to eat Spanish rice, I knew I would hear good news. And I always did! We shared a lot of good laughs eating it."

Every Christmas she invites friends to a tree-decorating party. The group of about 40 guests breaks into teams to hang ornaments that have been divided by color: green, red, gold, blue, and clear. Her guests, she says, mainly people in their sixties and seventies, with a few younger folks mixed in, are from all walks of life.

They may be judges, police officers, homemakers, academics, doctors, or businesspeople. Nevertheless, she says, the teams "get heated," each one trying to outdo the other with their decorating prowess. It's not a competition; just good fun accompanied by a lot of laughter and good-natured jostling. By the time the tree is hung with all its finery, everyone is ready for Dr. Angelou's homemade chili, cornbread, and ice-cold beer. The competitive spirit gives way and everyone unites over the delicious food.

More often, Dr. Angelou cooks for a few friends. One of her favorite simple meals is roast chicken with hot bread, but she also has a soft spot for a dish she first tasted about 30 years ago at the Algonquin Hotel in New York City. Called Spaghetti Caruso, it's made by lightly sautéing chicken livers in butter before adding them to tomato sauce. "The livers finish cooking in the sauce," she says, and cautions that you "don't want to cook them too long or they won't be tender."

When her mother and grandmother cooked, she recalls, it never seemed like work, and yet platters of food, beautifully presented, would appear on the table and uplift the spirits of guests. It's a precious lesson that she learned from the women in her family and that makes her own table a most welcoming one.

Maya Angelou's Recipe
■ **Banana Pudding** (page 262)

> "You feel special when you cook for others . . . And you feel special when it's done for you."

278

Chocolate-Dipped Biscotti

Chef: Jacques Torres

Go nuts for biscotti laced with almonds and pistachios
and dipped in bittersweet chocolate.

¾ cup whole almonds
⅓ cup shelled pistachios
¾ cup sugar
7 Tbsp. unsalted butter
2 large eggs
2 cups all-purpose flour
1 Tbsp. anise seeds
1 tsp. baking powder
1 ½ tsp. finely grated fresh lemon zest
Pinch of salt
1 large egg white, lightly beaten
12 ounces bittersweet chocolate,
    melted

1 Preheat oven to 300°. Place nuts on a large baking sheet and bake 25 to 30 minutes, or until toasted; cool.

2 In a large bowl, beat sugar, butter, and eggs on medium-high speed until smooth. Add flour, anise seeds, baking powder, zest, and salt. Stir in nuts. Shape dough into a disc; cover in plastic wrap and chill 1 hour.

3 Raise oven temperature to 350°. Divide dough into 3 equal pieces. On a lightly floured board, roll each piece into a log about 1 inch wide and 2 inches long. Line 2 cookie sheets with parchment paper. Arrange 2 logs on 1 cookie sheet, 3 inches apart, and the last on remaining sheet. Brush with egg white. Bake logs 30 minutes, placing cookie sheets in oven on middle rack and next rack above.

4 Remove and cool 10 minutes. Reduce oven to 300°. Cut logs on a slight angle into ½-inch-thick slices using a very sharp knife. Cut with a fast downward motion instead of dragging through log. (Large nuts will pull and crumble log.) Arrange biscotti on their sides and bake 10 to 12 minutes, until firm. Cool completely.

5 Horizontally dip biscotti halfway on a diagonal into melted chocolate. Arrange on their sides on a sheet of parchment or waxed paper and allow to dry. Store at room temperature in an airtight container with sheets of waxed paper between layers.

Makes about 5 dozen.

WHAT TO SERVE

What to Serve...

Port-Glazed Figs with Walnuts & Stilton (page 274)

Blueberry Buckle (page 250)

When You
Crave Something
Healthy

Heirloom Tomatoes with Lemon Tahini (page 26)

283

For the Vegetarians You Love

Callaloo (page 74)

A Celebration of Spring Vegetables (page 164)

Wine Pairings

"Serve red wine with meat and white with seafood" is one of those old-fashioned traditions that no longer applies to today's diverse and multi-ethnic food. If you feel like having a peppery Zinfandel with your salmon, go ahead. Drinking wine is about pleasing you. Whatever your choice, *salute!*

To help you decide what wine to try, Marco Pasanella of Pasanella and Sons Vintners in New York City offers some recommendations.

REDS
■ Medium-bodied and aromatic
African Chicken in Peanut Sauce (page 121) *Red Sancerre*
Beef Stew with Cognac & Horseradish Mustard (page 94) *Pommard, French red Burgundy*
Cabbage-Wrapped Salmon Steamed in Wine (page 150) *Poulsard*
Grilled Sesame-Marinated Duck Breasts with Hoisin Sauce (page 126) *Gevrey-Chambertin*
Moroccan Cinnamon-Rubbed Leg of Lamb (page 103) *Musigny, Burgundy*
Orange-Ginger Pork Medallions (page 98) *Samur-Charmigny, Red Burgundy*
Prosciutto di Parma–Black Pepper Quesadillas with Rosemary Oil (page 21) *Nero D'Avola, Southern Italy*

(Left to right) Cabbage-Wrapped Salmon Steamed in Wine (page 150), **Spaghetti Carbonara** (page 196), **Yogurt and Citrus Turkey Breast with Grilled Tomato & Wax Bean Salad** (page 134).

■ Earthy and dense
Bolognese Sauce with Pasta (page 194) *Rucche, Tuscan Red*
Lemon Pepper Dry-Rub Ribs with Garden Vegetable Barbecue Sauce (page 102) *Sonoma Petite Sirah*
Moroccan Chicken over Couscous (page 120) *Merlot*
Sausage Rolls with Worcestershire Sauce (page 17) *Dolcetto D'Alba*
Spaghetti Carbonara (page 196) *Barbera D'Alba Piedmont Red*
Spiced Butternut Squash & Apple Soup with Maple Pumpernickel Croutons (page 70) *Giacchè, Red Lazian*
Two Skillet Roasted Herbed Chicken with Oven Fries (page 122) *Carneros Zinfandel*
Yogurt and Citrus Turkey Breast with Grilled Tomato & Wax Bean Salad (page 134) *Carignano Blend, Sardinia*

■ Classic and full
Cornish Game Hens with Wild Rice & Mushroom Stuffing (page 130) *Châteauneuf-du-Pape*
Creole Gumbo (page 68) *Aglianico*
Cuban 24-Hour Roast Pork (page 100) *Ribera Del Duero*
Grilled Lamb Chops with Orange-Rosemary Rub & Grilled Vegetables (page 108) *Pauillac, Left Bank Bordeaux*
Rib Eye Steaks with Cornmeal-Fried Onion Rings (page 92) *Napa Merlot*
Organic Turkey Stuffed with Brown & Wild Rice, Dried Cranberries, & Walnuts (page 133) *Côte Rôtie*

287

What to Serve

WHITES

■ Light and crisp

Arugula & Barley Tabbouleh (page 202) *Fiano D'Avellino*

Beet Salad with Grilled Red Onions, Manouri Cheese, & Kalamata Vinaigrette (page 38) *Txacolina, Crisp Basque White*

Curried Cauliflower & Apple Soup with Cilantro Cream (page 69) *Kerner, Sylvaner*

Gazpacho Granita (page 10) *Albarion*

Spicy Shrimp with Basil (page 156) *Grüner Veltliner*

Tangy Autumn Greens with Tamari-Roasted Walnuts, Dried Cherries, & Stilton (page 34) *Pigato, Ligurian White*

■ Floral and aromatic

Buster Crab, Lettuce, & Tomato Po'boy (page 84) *Un-oaked Aligoté*

Grilled Skirt Steak Salad (page 90) *Washington State Cabernet Sauvignon*

Mango Couscous (page 202) *Alsatian Pinot Gris*

Oprah's Favorite Crab Cakes (page 157) *Sancerre Loire Sauvignon Blanc*

Poached Cod with Olive & Orange Vinaigrette (page 138) *Pouilly Fumé*

Seared Sea Scallops with Spicy Clementine Dipping Sauce (page 12) *Roero Arneis Tuscan White*

Stacked Tomato Salad (page 26) *Sauvignon Blanc from Santa Barbara*

Thai Chicken Coconut Curry Soup (page 72) *Vouvray*

Tomato Sandwich (page 79) *Long Island Riesling*

288

(Left to right) Crostini with Wild Mushrooms & Mozzarella (page 18), **Sweet Potato Salad** (page 32), **Beet Salad with Grilled Red Onions, Manouri Cheese, & Kalamata Vinaigrette** (page 38).

■ Full-bodied and buttery

Chicken & Pancetta Panini with Fontina, Arugula, & Provençal Mustard (page 86) *Jasnières*

Crostini with Wild Mushrooms & Mozzarella (page 18) *Mâcon, French White Burgundy*

Crushed Potato with Smoked Salmon, Caviar, & Chives (page 14) *Dry White Bordeaux*

Grilled Redfish with Red Rice & Lemon Butter Sauce (page 140) *Rueda*

Lemon-Olive Chicken with Vegetable Tagine (page 116) *Château-Grillet Rhone White*

Maine Lobster Acqua Pazza (page 160) *Savennières*

Panzanella (page 28) *Ribolla Gialla Friulian Full-Bodied White Pinot Noir*

Seared Tuna with Fresh Corn & Wasabi "Cream" (page 142) *Montrachet White Burgundy*

Sweet Corn Salad with Black Beans, Scallions, & Tomatoes (page 30) *Sonoma Chardonnay*

Sweet Potato Salad (page 32) *Riesling*

Swordfish Niçoise (page 144) *Chablis*

■ Other great choices

Chutney Chicken Salad Tea Sandwiches (page 81) *Champagne*

Gnocchi with Fall Sage Pesto (page 192) *Sercial Madeira*

Mint & Pea Hummus with Pita Bread (page 24) *Prosecco – Light & Minerally*

About the Chefs & Contributors

Mollie Ahlstrand is chef and owner of the Italian restaurant Trattoria Mollie in Montecito, California.

Maya Angelou is a poet, educator, historian, best-selling author, actress, playwright, civil rights activist, producer, director, and one of the great voices of contemporary literature.

Govind Armstrong is author of *Small Bites, Big Nights* and head chef at the Table 8 restaurants in Miami and Los Angeles.

Lee Bailey was an award-winning chef, entertaining expert, and author of the best-selling lifestyle and entertaining book *Lee Bailey's Country Weekends*.

Dan Barber is chef and co-owner of Blue Hill restaurant in New York City and Blue Hill at Stone Barns in Pocantico Hills, New York.

Celia Barbour, *O*'s contributing food editor, has also written about food for the *New York Times*, *Gourmet*, *Food and Wine*, and elsewhere.

John Besh is a James Beard Foundation Award recipient and owner of the restaurants *Lüke*, *Restaurant August*, *La Provence*, and *Besh Steak* in Louisiana.

Tom Bivins is executive chef for the Montpelier campus of the New England Culinary Institute.

April Bloomfield, who was named one of the Best Chefs in 2007 by *Food & Wine*, is executive chef and co-owner of The Spotted Pig in New York City.

Jim Botsacos is head chef of Molyvos Restaurant in New York City and author of *The New Greek Cuisine*.

Daniel Boulud is a James Beard Foundation Award–winning chef, author of *Braise: A Journey Through International Cuisine* and five other cookbooks, and owner of the famous restaurant Daniel in New York City as well as restaurants in Palm Beach, Miami, and Las Vegas.

Ralph Brennan owns the restaurants Red Fish Grill, Bacco, and Ralph's on the Park in New Orleans, and Ralph Brennan's Jazz Kitchen at the Disneyland Resort.

Sheila Bridges is CEO and Chairperson of Sheila Bridges Design Inc., an interior design company based in New York City. Her work has been featured in *Time*, *New York Magazine*, the *New York Times*, and the *Wall Street Journal*.

Leah Chase, head chef of Dooky Chase Restaurant in New Orleans since the mid-1950s, is author of *And Still I Cook* and *The Dooky Chase Cookbook*.

Olivier Cheng is chef and owner of Olivier Cheng Catering and Events in New York City.

Susan Chumsky is a New York City–based writer who has contributed to *O*, *Entertainment Weekly*, *The New Yorker*, and *Real Simple*.

Patrice Clayton is owner of The Harlem Tea Room in New York City.

Pino Coladonato is chef and owner of La Masseria, an Italian restaurant in New York City.

Colin Cowie, a South African–born expert on entertaining, is an event planner and author of five books including his latest, *Colin Cowie Chic: The Guide to Life As It Should Be*.

Norma Jean Darden, a native of North Carolina, is author of *Spoonbread and Strawberry Wine* and owner of Miss Mamie's and Miss Maude's restaurants in New York City.

Paula Disbrowe is a chef and author of *Cowgirl Cuisine: Rustic Recipes and Cowgirl Adventures from a Texas Ranch*.

Bobby Flay is owner and executive chef of five restaurants in New York City, Las Vegas, Atlantic City, and the Bahamas. He has hosted several shows on the Food Network and is author of ten cookbooks, including the upcoming *Bobby Flay's Grill It!*

Andrew Friedman is a food writer and author of a cookbook called *Chef on a Shoestring*, as well as co-author of several cookbooks with chefs Michael Lomonaco, Alfred Portale, Bill Telepan, and Laurent Tourondel.

Gale Gand hosted the Food Network's *Sweet Dreams* and is author of six cookbooks including *Short & Sweet* and *Chocolate & Vanilla*.

Ina Garten is a chef, host of the Food Network's program *Barefoot Contessa*, and author of several cookbooks including *Barefoot Contessa at Home*.

Suzanne Goin is chef and owner of the restaurants Lucques, A.O.C., and The Hungry Cat in Los Angeles. She is author of the cookbook *Sunday Suppers at Lucques*.

Rozanne Gold is an award-winning chef, author, and restaurant consultant based in New York City. Her latest book is *Kids Cook 1-2-3*.

Moira Hodgson is restaurant critic for the *New York Observer* and author of the cookbook *Favorite Fruitcakes*.

Melissa Kelly, a James Beard Foundation Award winner, is executive chef and co-owner of Primo restaurant in Rockland, Maine.

Gayle King is editor at large of *O* and host of *The Gayle King Show* on XM Satellite Radio.

Peggy Knickerbocker is a food writer, consulting editor for *Saveur* and *Gourmet*, and author of five cookbooks. Her work has also appeared in *Food & Wine*, the *New York Times*, and the *Los Angeles Times*.

Price Kushner is pastry chef and co-owner of Primo restaurant in Rockland, Maine.

Edna Lewis was a chef and leading proponent of Southern cooking. She was also the author of several cookbooks including *A Taste of Country Cooking*.

Joyce Maynard is author of the memoir *At Home in the World*. She teaches pie workshops at her home in Mill Valley, California.

Julia McClaskey is a chef based in San Francisco.

Colleen McGlynn is owner of DaVero Olive Oils and Supper, a prepared foods business based in Sonoma County, California.

Alice Medrich is a teacher, chef, author, and chocolate expert. Her latest book is *Pure Dessert: True Flavors, Inspiring Ingredients, and Simple Recipes*.

Alison Mesrop is a chef and owner of Alison B. Mesrop Catering in New York City.

Gail Monaghan is a New York City–based cookbook author, editor, and cooking teacher. Her latest cookbook is called *Lost Desserts*.

Michelle Myers is an award-winning pastry chef at Sona restaurant in Los Angeles.

Cary Neff is a chef and author of the cookbook *Conscious Cuisine*.

Michel Nischan is a renowned chef, award-winning cookbook author, and proponent of sustainable foods and agriculture. His cookbooks include *Homegrown: Pure & Simple* and *Taste: Pure & Simple*.

Marco Pasanella is founder and owner of Pasanella and Son, a New York City-based wine shop.

Laura Pensiero is a French Culinary Institute graduate, registered dietitian, restaurateur, and author. She founded and operates Chef4life, a nutrition and culinary consulting service that promotes healthy eating

Mimi Pond is a cartoonist and writer based in Los Angeles. She is author of several humor books, most recently *Splitting Hairs: The Bald Truth About Bad Hair Days*.

Debra Ponzek is a chef, author of three cookbooks, and owner of the café and food shop Aux Délices in Riverside, Connecticut. Her latest cookbook is *The Family Kitchen*.

Susan Quick is senior food editor at *Health* magazine. She is also author of *Quick Simple Food* and *Go Bananas! 150 Recipes for America's Most Versatile Fruit.*

Nadia Roden is an award-winning artist, designer, and author of *Granita Magic*. A native Londoner, she now lives in New York City.

Marcus Samuelsson is chef and co-owner of Aquavit restaurant in New York City, and author of *The Soul of a New Cuisine*.

Nina Simonds is an award-winning author of ten books on Asian food and culture. She is a regular contributor to *O* and also writes for the *New York Times* as well as other national publications.

Margaux Sky is the owner of Art Café and Bakery in San Luis Obispo, California. She is also author of *Beautiful Breads and Fabulous Fillings*.

Art Smith is a two-time James Beard Foundation Award recipient, chef, author, and television personality. He is author of several cookbooks including *Back to the Table*, *Kitchen Life*, and *Back to the Family*.

Larry Smith is head baker at Mister Smith's Bakery, Café & Catering in Vermillion, South Dakota.

Joachim Splichal is an award-winning chef and owner of Patina Restaurant in Los Angeles in addition to five French bistro–style restaurants in Southern California and Las Vegas.

Susan Spungen is a chef, food editor, and co-author of the best-selling *Recipes: A Collection for the Modern Cook*.

Matt Steigerwald is executive chef and owner of the Lincoln Café in Mount Vernon, Iowa.

Bill Telepan is chef and owner of the New York City restaurant Telepan. He is the co-author with Andrew Friedman of a cookbook called *Inspired by Ingredients: Market Menus and Family Favorites from a Three-Star Chef.*

Mary Jo Thoresen and her husband, Curt Clingman, are chefs and co-owners of Jojo, a French bistro in Oakland, California.

Jacques Torres is pastry chef and owner of Jacques Torres Chocolate and Chocolate Haven, both in New York City.

Rori Trovato is a New York City–based chef and the author of several cookbooks including *Dishing with Style*.

Andre Walker is a world-renowned hairstylist and Oprah Winfrey's hairdresser. He is the author of *Andre Talks Hair*.

Jody Williams is executive chef at Morandi Restaurant in New York City.

290

Photography Credits

Cover: **top left** Antonis Achilleos; **top center** Ann Stratton; **top right** Tina Rupp; **bottom** Tina Rupp; **Inside flap** Sang An; **Endpaper** Gentl and Hyers; **Page 3** Ann Stratton; **4 top left** Maria Robledo; **4 top center** Anna Williams; **4 top right** Richard Gerhard Jung; **4 middle left** Ann Stratton; **4 middle center** Anna Williams; **4 middle right** Anna Williams; **4 bottom left** Tina Rupp; **4 bottom center** Rita Maas; **4 bottom right** Richard Gerhard Jung; **5** Jim Franco **6** Matthew Rolston; **8** Anna Williams; **11** Gentl and Hyers; **13** Ann Stratton; **15** John Kernick; **17** James Baigrie; **19** Ann Stratton; **20** Anna Williams; **21** Evan Sklar; **23** Antonis Achilleos; **25** John Kernick; **27** Anna Williams; **29** Maria Robledo; **30** Marcus Nilsson; **31** Marcus Nilsson; **33** Ann Stratton; **35** Ann Stratton; **37** Anna Williams; **39** Richard Gerhard Jung; **40** Jim Franco; **43 top** Hayley Harrison; **bottom** John Kernick; **45** John Kernick; **46** Hayley Harrison; **47** James Baigrie; **49** Sang An; **51** Gentl and Hyers; **53** Ann Stratton; **54** Sang An; **57** Ann Stratton; **61** John Kernick; **63** Ann Stratton; **65** Richard Gerhard Jung; **67** Gentl and Hyers; **68** Francesco Lagnese **71** Maria Robledo; **73** Richard Gerhard Jung; **75** Anna Williams; **77** Gentl and Hyers; **81** Gentl and Hyers; **83** Gentl and Hyers; **85** Francesco Lagnese; **87** Gentl and Hyers; **88** Quentin Bacon; **90** Tina Rupp; **95** Gentl and Hyers; **97** Antonis Achilleos; **99** Gentl and Hyers; **101** Jim Franco; **103** Ann Stratton; **105** Ann Stratton; **109** Tina Rupp; **111** Richard Gerhard Jung; **112** Victoria Pearson; **117** Anna Williams; **119** Ann Stratton; **120** William Meppem ; **121** Maura McEvoy; **123** Anna Williams;

125 Ann Stratton; **127** Marcus Nilsson; **129** Shimon and Tammar; **131** Amy Neunsinger; **135** Gentl and Hyers; **136** Maria Robledo; **139** John Kernick; **141** Francesco Lagnese; **143** Ann Stratton; **145** Quentin Bacon; **147** Beatriz Da Costa; **149** Gentl and Hyers; **151** Gentl and Hyers; **153** Gentl and Hyers; **155** Shimon and Tammar; **159** Marcus Nilsson; **161** Anna Williams; **162** Sang An; **165** Shimon and Tammar; **167** John Kernick; **169** Shimon and Tammar; **171** Maria Robledo; **173** Gentl and Hyers; **175** Jonelle Weaver; **177** Tina Rupp; **179** Tina Rupp; **181** Maria Robledo; **182** Anna Williams; **185** Ann Stratton; **187** Gentl and Hyers; **189** Shimon and Tammar; **191** Richard Gerhard Jung; **193** Richard Gerhard Jung; **195** Tara Donne; **197** Sang An; **199** William Meppem; **201** Amy Neunsinger; **205** Anna Williams; **206** Anna Williams; **211** Shimon and Tammar; **213** Anna Williams; **214** Maria Robledo; **216** Henry Leutwyler; **217** Hayley Harrison; **219** Shimon and Tammar; **221** Maria Robledo; **223** Gentl and Hyers; **227** Monica Buck; **229** Maura McEvoy; **230** Maria Robledo; **232** Tina Rupp; **235** Rita Maas; **237** Luca Trovato; **239** Richard Gerhard Jung; **241** Tina Rupp; **243** Ann Stratton; **245** Shimon and Tammar; **247** John Kernick; **249** Amy Neunsinger; **251** John Kernick; **253** Ann Stratton; **255** Gentl and Hyers; **257** Rita Maas; **259** John Kernick; **260** Ann Stratton; **261** James Baigrie; **263** Tina Rupp; **265** Anna Williams; **267** Maura McEvoy; **268** Gentl and Hyers; **269** Sang An; **271** Gentl and Hyers; **273** Kirsten Strecker; **275** Richard Gerhard Jung; **277** Anna Williams; **279** Maura McEvoy; **Back cover** Henry Leutwyler

Index

293

298

299

300

301

303